The Spirit of Christopher

The Spirit of Christopher

A Bereaved Parent Shares Hope After the Tragic Loss of Her Child

CAROL MACEY

Copyright © 2022 Carol Macey

All rights reserved. No part of this publication may be reproduced or transmitted, in any form or by any means, without written permission of the publisher except for the use of quotations in a citation.

To request permission, contact the publisher at:
publisher@innerpeacepress.com

ISBN: 978-1-7351738-4-9

The Spirit of Christopher: **A Bereaved Parent Shares Hope After the Tragic Loss of Her Child**

Paperpack
March 2022

Subjects:
Grief & Bereavement
Mental Health
Parenting & Relationships

Published by Inner Peace Press
Eau Claire, Wisconsin, USA
www.innerpeacepress.com

This is for you Elizabeth, my beautiful daughter and Christopher's sister, who has been through this journey with me. All my love and hugs always, Mum xxxxxx

To my wonderful husband Stephen who has been there for me even though you never knew Christopher. Love you so much, Carol xxxxxx

A special thank you to Julia Robinson who helped me with this book in the early days and Sadie Colyer who has seen me through to the end of the journey of finally publishing *The Spirit of Christopher*.

Table of Contents

Introduction		9
Chapter 1:	8 October 2006	13
Chapter 2:	The "Spirit" of Christopher	21
Chapter 3:	The Funeral	43
Chapter 4:	Psychosis	51
Chapter 5:	The First Six Months	65
Chapter 6:	Green Shoots and Black Clouds	79
Chapter 7:	Elizabeth	95
Chapter 8:	A New Normal	109
Chapter 9:	8 October 2016	117
Chapter 10:	Therapy	123
Chapter 11:	What I Have Gained From Writing This Book	129
Chapter 12:	Managing My Grief The Bereaved Parent	135
For Those Who Won't Ask		143
Resources		145
About the Author		148

Introduction

My name is Carol and I'm a mental health nurse and life coach. Thank you for picking up this book, which tells the story of my son Christopher's battle with mental illness. He experienced his first psychotic episode at age 19, when I was a mature student studying for a diploma in nursing. Sadly, despite the best efforts of his friends, family, and mental health team, Christopher continued to deteriorate over the next ten years until his death from liver failure at age 29.

The book also describes how our family coped with the aftermath and how my professional self has helped me process some of the events.

I have wanted to write this book for a long time. Partly to commemorate his life and leave a legacy to friends and family, but also to share some of the things I have learned along the way. This book is also for other bereaved parents, or those whose loved ones are dealing with severe mental illness. I need you to understand that I am not a writer; this is my experience in its raw form that I wanted to share with others.

When I began writing I wasn't really sure what to include – it was just something I needed to do. Perhaps to transfigure my sadness into something positive, perhaps to bring meaning to his life, or to give hope to other bereaved parents. In doing so, I also wanted to raise awareness and reduce the stigma currently surrounding mental health issues. Perhaps I could even help someone better understand a child or family member with an ongoing and serious mental health problem.

Losing my child was completely unexpected and something I never thought I would have to face. Being predeceased by one's child is generally thought of as one of the worst things that can happen to a parent – a violation of the way events are supposed to occur. When Christopher passed away on 8 October 2006, I thought I would never get through it. There was no instruction manual, I didn't even know how I was supposed to grieve for him.

But somehow I found the inner strength to go on and to create a "new normal" without Christopher, even if I made an awful lot of mistakes along the way. Severe mental illness is never logical and it is often impossible to process the fallout from a young life interrupted by it. Although each family's story is unique, through my work – currently in a team dealing with early onset of psychosis in individuals aged 14 to 65 – I see again and again how the same themes appear: alcoholism and substance abuse, isolation and lack of insight.

Not everyone reading this book will be able to identify with what I have written. I have exposed parts of myself that people may find difficult to understand, but I needed to do this in order to be true to myself. In sharing my journey, I hope I have created a legacy for my beautiful boy, and in doing so inspire others to continue their journey, whatever stage they may be at. I have been told I'm brave. I don't think so. I simply do whatever all bereaved parents have to do to get through each day without Christopher in my life. But in my new normal, he is always in my heart and beside me in spirit. Daily his spirit informs my nursing and life coaching. I hope my words will bring you comfort for your own grief, or perhaps help you understand someone else who is going through a similar situation.

Christopher (age 28) enjoying a night out the year before he passed

Chapter 1

~

8 October 2006

It was the morning after the night from hell. I had been to a 40th birthday party in Bristol and someone had unplugged my phone from the outlet and the battery was completely flat. Annoyed, I left it charging while we went out for breakfast, not remembering to switch it on until I started the drive home, around 3 PM.

And then the bombshell hit. A message from my father left at 8 AM that morning. Christopher had collapsed and was now in Medway Hospital with a suspected paracetamol overdose.

Listening to his message I felt like someone had stabbed me – I had been out enjoying myself while my son was in the hospital. As I phoned my dad, my heart was pounding. I had no idea what to expect.

"Carol, I've been trying to contact you all day," he said. "Christopher is in the hospital, they think he's taken a paracetamol overdose."

This didn't make sense. Although Christopher had been very ill recently, I knew he would not deliberately take an overdose. He had a strong Catholic faith and suicide would have been absolutely taboo. If anything, I was expecting to hear he had been sectioned under the Mental Health Act.

"Is he ok?" I asked.

"I think so," Dad replied, "he's having some tests done.

I found him collapsed at the bottom of the stairs this morning, so I phoned for an ambulance. I phoned Mary and she's at the hospital with him."

Mary was Christopher's paternal grandmother. My dad, Norman, a little older than Mary, was becoming quite frail. Having found Christopher must have been a terrible shock for him. I guess that was why he didn't go in the ambulance with Christopher.

When I phoned the hospital, the doctor seemed more concerned about Christopher's mental rather than his physical state. Christopher was being aggressive and threatening to discharge himself; he hated hospitals. The doctor tried to reassure me that Christopher was ok and stable. She even told me not to worry and that there was no need to rush back – obviously she didn't want me speeding on the motorway! I felt comforted that Mary had gone straight to the hospital and was now with him.

When I eventually got to the hospital it was around 6 PM. Mary had already left so I approached one of the nurses and asked where Christopher was. He told me that the doctor wanted to talk to me before I saw him. I was confused – something was wrong. I kept asking why I couldn't see Christopher, but was simply told I needed to see the doctor first.

As I waited, I felt a suffocating sense of dread. Why wouldn't they let me see Christopher? I remember phoning my partner, Mitch (not his real name), who was parking the car. We had been together for 13 years and he had been a big part of Christopher's life.

Just as Mitch arrived on the ward, the doctor approached. She took me into a side room and told me Christopher had suffered a heart attack and tests indicated his liver was failing. The staff were trying to find a bed for him in a liver unit. This was a complete shock. They had lied to me! Whenever I had spoken to the nursing staff on my drive back they told me Christopher was fine. I had no indication that anything was seriously wrong, not physically at any rate.

"Is my son going to die?" I asked.

"I can't tell you that," she replied.

"Of course you can. You just don't want to commit yourself. Can I see my son please?"

The doctor took me to a room where Christopher was lying unconscious. He was wired up to several monitors, a hospital gown covering the lower part of his body. I held his hand, feeling sick and afraid. I could see things weren't good from the blood pressure monitor. I desperately wanted everything to be ok. I wanted him to wake up, so I could tell him how much I loved him. Please no, this couldn't be happening.

The nurse who was looking after Christopher encouraged me to talk to him and she reassured me that he could hear what I was saying. Christopher was lying unnaturally still with an oxygen mask over his mouth. I told him I loved him – it was important he knew. I don't know why but I then started waffling about my approaching 50th birthday and how his sister, Elizabeth, was going to arrange a party for me.

I had to leave the room while the medical staff carried out some further tests. As I did so I saw my friend Christine walking up the corridor. I met Christine in 2005 at a school where I was working as a Community Psychiatric Nurse. She was the school nurse and we worked well as a team and ended up becoming close friends. I had phoned her on my way home from Bristol to tell her that Christopher was in the hospital. She gave me a hug.

"I had to come," she said, "I knew something was wrong."

My best friend Sue and her husband Malc arrived soon after. Her son was the same age as Christopher and we first met at the school gate when our sons started school together. I was so glad she was there too.

Christopher was taken to have a liver scan. While he was gone, I went to the hospital chapel. My brave, wonderful young man was dying. I hadn't prayed in years, not since my mum died. In the years since, my beliefs have become less traditionally religious and more spiritual in nature. Although I wasn't sure who or what I was praying to, it seemed the right thing to do. "Please God, if you are going to let him live, please don't let him continue to suffer the way he has. If you can't stop his torment and pain, then please take him and give him the peace he deserves."

I knew I was asking a lot of God – and myself – but I knew the outcome was out of my hands. I went back to be with my son.

When the doctor called me back into her room, I knew the die was cast. Instead of asking again if Christopher was going to die, I asked, "How long has he got?"

She shook her head, "I'm afraid it's only a matter of hours."

I asked one of the nurses if I should phone for the Catholic priest or leave it for a bit longer. He spoke very softly, "I would contact him now."

I then phoned Christopher's sister Elizabeth, my dad, and Con's parents Mary and Mick to tell them what was happening. I can't really remember anything about the conversations I had with them. Mary asked me if I had called for the priest and I reassured her that he was on his way. Christopher's dad, Con, was working abroad and there was no way of getting hold of him. Con and I separated in July 1994, but things between us were finally very amicable.

Minutes later Elizabeth, my dad, and Mary were on their way to say goodbye to Christopher. I was grateful that Sue and Malc had gone to fetch them as soon as I was told the news. When they arrived, Christopher was receiving the last rites from the priest. Shortly afterwards, alarm bells began ringing and members of the medical team came rushing from everywhere. Christopher had gone into cardiac arrest and there was nothing they could do. I heard a voice pronounce him dead. It was 10 PM.

Elizabeth and I went into the room where Christopher had died. The medical team all turned to look at us. I asked the staff to leave us alone, "Elizabeth and I want to be alone with my son," I said.

In hindsight, I was being extremely rude and bad mannered but I needed to see him so desperately. Elizabeth stood at the end of the bed, silent tears running down her face. My poor girl. If I could have taken her pain away, I would have. I knew Christopher was at peace, but if you had asked me what I was feeling, I couldn't tell you. I felt there was an invisible protective cloak wrapped around me to block the pain. Without it, I think I would have gone mad. Thankfully the cloak did its job well for the next few days.

While they were removing the monitors and tidying up Christopher's body, we all made our way to the hospital lounge. The nurses were wonderful. They were so kind and made us all tea. My dad looked in a state of shock. For the first time ever, he had started to look his age. Christopher had been living with him at the end and my dad had taken really good care of him, but now someone needed to support my dad. I spoke to the doctor about my concerns. She was lovely and went to talk to him. He really appreciated that and started to tell her all about Christopher. Mary thanked me for making sure that her beloved grandson had received the last rights, which was important to her as a Catholic. I knew it would have been important to Christopher, too. It was my first priority when I knew he was going to die.

Although I didn't practice any particular faith, I knew Christopher's belief in God was absolute. I suddenly noticed

Elizabeth was missing. When I found her, she was sitting on the floor in the hospital corridor outside the ward. She was crying on the phone to her best friend. She looked so young and vulnerable. This was all so unfair on her. The decision to leave the hospital that night was the hardest I've ever had to make. To leave Christopher there in that dark, sterile ward all alone with strangers broke my heart. As I stood by his bedside, I bent down to kiss him and told him I loved him. "You will always be in my heart Christopher," I whispered.

Long after Mitch had gone to bed, I sat in silence alone with my thoughts. Trying to make sense of what had transpired. At 3 AM something amazing happened. The room in which I was sitting suddenly felt strangely warm and was filled with a glowing white light – as if I was surrounded by angels – and I knew that my beautiful boy was starting his journey to heaven. He had come to tell me that he was at peace. I woke Mitch and called him to come downstairs.

"Can you feel it? Look at the room, it's all lit up," I marveled.

"I'm not meant to feel it," he replied.

I was surprised he couldn't feel or sense anything. But as he went back upstairs, I realized he was right. It felt like a message from Christopher to let me know he was ok. He stayed for about half an hour. I felt such an overwhelming sense of peace and love. When the time finally came for him to leave me, I felt his spirit touch me and I knew Christopher would never be very far away. Sometimes I feel a soft wind brush across my cheek and I know he is beside me.

Me with Christopher (age 2 and a half) at Rochester Castle enjoying a moment of quiet

Chapter 2

~

The "Spirit" of Christopher

I first met Con when I was 15 and he was going out with one of my school friends. That relationship didn't last long, but he always seemed to be in the background. At the time I was going out with someone a lot older than me and in constant battles with my mum about it. It was the first time I really went against her. I spent a lot of time with my older cousins and wanted to be like them, so when I eventually stopped dating him, she was so relieved.

Although most of my friends were having sex, I just wasn't ready and didn't give in to the taunts about still being a virgin. When Con asked me out when I was 17, I still hadn't experienced a sexual relationship. He was nearer my age and so mum approved. It was a bit of a false start because he had been seeing a girl from the Midlands and she only came down to see him on the weekends. Although they had argued, it was unclear whether it had ended. Eventually Con spoke to her about things that were none of my business and decided to finish with her. So, we became an "item."

One of the things I first noticed about Con was that he was always smartly dressed and took great care of his appearance. At that time, he was often mistaken for the man out of the pop group Dollar mainly because of his hair style. He was always very respectful and polite. My previous boyfriend had been a bit of a "bad boy" and never worried about how he looked, so it was a complete contrast. Con had a cheeky sense of humor that really appealed to me. At 17 I was starting to become quite curious about sex. After a few fumbles, Con and I eventually had sex for the first time. We were both so naive and never discussed contraception. I was too scared to go on the pill in case my mum found them. This had happened to a friend of mine and the repercussions had been awful. I just never thought I would get pregnant.

My journey began in the autumn of 1976 when I discovered I was pregnant. I was just 18 years old and engaged to be married to Con. The pregnancy had come as a shock to us both and we were terrified to tell our parents. In the 1970s it was still not socially acceptable to have a baby out of wedlock, added to this my own mother had a very Victorian attitude towards sex outside of marriage. It was just something you didn't do.

The day had come for me to phone up for my pregnancy test results. In those days there was no such thing as going to buy a home pregnancy test in Boots (a pharmacy). I had to wait five long days after taking a urine sample into the doctor's office. That evening after finishing work I walked to the telephone box at the bottom of Darnley Road in Strood to make the call that was going to change my life. The booth smelled strongly of stale urine and I found myself retching. It was late August but I couldn't tell you what the weather was like.

My friend Jackie was with me and she was convinced it was a false alarm and I had nothing to worry about. But the changes in my body told me differently. My boobs were very tender and I hadn't had a period for nearly two months. Usually my periods were so regular, four weeks to the day! How I longed to feel that familiar monthly cramp that told me my period had started. As I dialed the telephone number of the doctor's office, I could feel my heart pounding. I heard a voice on the end of the telephone, "Good evening, Darnley Road Surgery."

I hesitated, and then said, "I've telephoned for my pregnancy results."

"What's your name dear?"

"Carol Dolling," I replied.

A few seconds went by.

"It's positive."

She said it so matter-of-factly and obviously had no idea of the implications of what she had just told me. I hung up.

I turned around to my friend, "Jackie, I'm pregnant," I said. She looked at me in disbelief.

"I'd better go, I need to face my mum and she's going to go bloody mad."

It was a long walk home. Darnley Road had always been a busy road and full of activity. Children playing while their mums stood on the doorstep, chatting and putting the world to rights. But in my bewildered state I was unaware of anything other than getting home to face my mum with the news that she was about to become a grandmother.

As I put my key in the door, I felt sick. I had decided to face my mum head on. There was no point waiting for the right time to tell her because there was never going to be one. As I walked into the kitchen, I saw mum standing by the sink. I could see on her face that she knew there was something wrong.

"Mum please sit down, I have something to tell you," I said. I was so nervous.

"What is it?" She was refusing to sit down. She seemed void of any emotion.

"Mum, I'm pregnant," I replied.

"You bloody little fool," she shouted.

She was so disappointed in me. As her only child she had always put me on a giant pedestal and I had just fallen off, big time.

"What are you going to do with it?" Her face was ashen. She was so angry.

"I don't know," I replied with effort.

"I think you should have an abortion," she said. I was shocked into silence.

I couldn't believe what I was hearing. Mum was so anti-abortion and here she was telling me to have one. My brother had been stillborn at full term twelve years earlier and she had never really gotten over it. Surely she didn't want me to kill my baby?

"I don't want an abortion Mum," I said quietly.

To be honest I wasn't sure what I did want, but I was very certain that I didn't want an abortion.

"Does Con know?" she asked.

"He's going to phone me tonight to find out the results."

"Well, if you're not going to have an abortion then you will have to get married," she sneered.

I wasn't sure I wanted that either. At that moment my dad came in from work.

"She's pregnant." My mum had said it with venom. He looked stunned.

"For heaven's sake," he cried.

"I've told her to have an abortion," Mum spat.

"She's not having an abortion, she is fit and healthy, and there is no reason for her to get rid of the baby," my dad shouted with alarm.

My parents were talking about me as if I wasn't in the room! The added complication, of course, was that Con's family were Catholic and very anti-abortion. While they were discussing my future, I knew my dad was thinking of his stillborn son. Mum was thinking about what other people would say about her precious daughter being pregnant outside marriage, but that's how it was in those days. Living with the stigma would have been unbearable. The situation was so difficult for her and her reaction wasn't meant to be as unkind or heartless as it seemed. An abortion would have gotten rid of the problem without people knowing.

Although attitudes towards unmarried mothers were very slowly beginning to change in the 70s, there was still a lot of stigma surrounding women who had babies out of wedlock. They were still being coerced into giving up their babies for adoption. Mother and baby homes were a response to social attitudes in the 50s, 60s, and 70s. In 1976 pregnant teenagers in the UK were still being forced to go to mother and baby homes by horrified parents to hide their pregnancies from friends and family. Babies were cruelly taken out of the arms of young teenage mothers and put into care. Adoption of the babies was then arranged through mainly church run agencies. Thankfully that didn't happen to me.

The phone rang and mum went to answer it. It was Con.

"Well you know what I think of you, don't you?" Mum ranted.

I didn't even have a chance to tell Con myself.

In the end it was my father who made the choice for me. He didn't believe in abortion and I didn't want one either, so a wedding was quickly arranged for me. Six weeks later, on 9 October 1976, I became Mrs. Carol Ring. After the wedding Con moved in with me in my mum and dad's house until our own new house was ready. My pregnancy was fairly straightforward, but it felt like it was happening to someone else.

As a teenager about to be thrust into motherhood after a shotgun wedding, I struggled to cope. I had started to feel depressed when I was pregnant. During the final months I suffered terrible heartburn and wasn't sleeping well. Con was away working and only came home on the weekends. I was still living with Mum and Dad, so nothing had really changed since our wedding.

Often my pregnancy didn't seem real. I went into labour on 19 April 1977, but didn't realize it, even though I was four days overdue. I had been up all night with diarrhea and a really bad backache. At 6 AM my mum called out to me. I didn't want to believe it and remember feeling terrified – this couldn't be happening, I wasn't ready. It didn't help that my mum was panicking and I was unable to get hold of Con, who was working in Leeds. Eventually I left a message with his head office, who promised to get the message to him.

The ambulance arrived to take me to hospital about 8 AM. I was having contractions in my back and naively still doubted I was in labour. I had always been told that you only get contractions in your stomach. My dad came with me; he was always the calm one out of my parents. When we arrived at the hospital the midwife confirmed I was in labour.

My dad asked if he could stay with me because Con wasn't able to be there. The midwife told him that only husbands were allowed to be at the birth. When my dad left, I wanted to call after him, "please don't leave me Dad, I can't do this on my own," but I stayed silent. It had always been my dad who I had turned to when I was upset, he was always so good at making everything seem better. I understand it was hospital policy regarding husbands, but even now it seems so cruel!

After he had gone, I was taken into a room and given an enema. Nobody had warned me about that. In those days, giving a labouring mother an enema wasn't a matter of choice but rather a standard, routinely administered in early labour as part of the hospital admission procedure. Apparently, the theory behind giving an enema in early labour is that emptying the bowels before delivery eliminates the possibility of waste matter in the rectum hindering the baby's descent through the birth canal, therefore preventing contamination of the sterile birthing field. Thankfully, today expectant mothers are now given the choice. I found the whole experience very degrading. The room was so cold and clinical. I must have been on the toilet for about twenty minutes before I was able to get into the bath. Suddenly I found myself needing the loo again. It was horrible. Just as I sat on the loo again the midwife came in.

"Haven't you showered yet?" she asked.

I felt very young and vulnerable. Close to tears, I found myself apologizing.

"Well hurry up," she said, "I'll be back soon to take you to the labour suite."

Once in the labour suite, I was praying it would all soon be over. I felt so lonely and scared. I was left on my own for what seemed like hours. From time to time a midwife came in to check on me. I was informed that Con had been tracked down and was on his way home.

Around 3 PM a doctor came into the room with a young, pretty midwife. "I don't like this, your labour is progressing too slowly," he said after a few minutes. "I'm going to put you on a drip to speed things up."

When the drip was put into my arm the midwife got splashed with my blood. She and the doctor began to laugh, she joked he had done it deliberately. They were flirting as if I wasn't in the room! I thought Con would be here by now, I had no idea what was taking him so long. Well, I thought, at least the drip would speed things up.

Someone had told me that once she had the drip in her arm, she gave birth within an hour. Unfortunately, I wasn't so fortunate. It was a long and lonely labour. I eventually gave birth to Christopher at 8 PM.

Suddenly the midwife was putting my baby into my arms. I didn't know how to hold him, it didn't seem real and I handed him straight back to her! The midwife looked quite bewildered. I just laid back on the bed feeling exhausted. There were no mobile phones in those days so I couldn't even phone my parents. I'd just given birth to a healthy baby boy; it really should have been the happiest time of my life, but I just felt overwhelmed by everything.

"We need to take the baby away and weigh him. Have you got a name for him yet?" the midwife asked.

"Christopher," I replied softly, I knew that part was right.

"I'll bring Christopher back as soon as we have checked him over," the midwife replied and swiftly whisked my newborn away.

I'd had an episiotomy during labour and needed stitches. I remember being trussed up like a chicken while the doctor sewed me back up. Who said having a baby was supposed to be a joyous occasion? It seemed to take ages. My body felt like public property. I don't remember much else until Con walked into the labour suite with the biggest smile on his face. He was the proudest father ever, but I just felt numb. Mentally and physically.

As a teenager suddenly thrust into motherhood, I struggled to cope or bond with my baby son. The feelings of exhaustion didn't lift and, looking back, I realised I was suffering from postpartum depression. According to the mental health foundation, this is very common among teenage mothers and is often associated with feelings of loneliness and low self-esteem. I can certainly relate to that. When Christopher was six weeks old, we moved into our own home and my depression somehow became worse.

While we lived with Mum and Dad, my only concern was caring for Chris. Now I had to learn how to run a house and everything that went with it, including cooking and cleaning. I just wanted to go back home to my parents where it felt safe.

Before too long, I found a disturbing way to take back control of my body. During my pregnancy I had gained a lot of weight and I continued to put it on after Christopher was born. A few people, rather surprisingly, made comments about it which lowered my self-esteem even more. I decided to lose weight. At first, I just cut down my portion sizes and tried to eat more healthily. As I began to lose weight, I started to feel better about myself. It was the one thing in my life I had control over. As a result, I bought lots of diet magazines and began looking for low calorie foods to include in my diet. If I'm honest, I was always hungry and food was constantly on my mind, but all I could think about was losing more weight. Whenever Con and I were invited out for lunch or dinner I would make myself sick after eating. I couldn't bear the thought of putting any of the weight back on. I began weighing myself every day and if I had gained any weight, I would restrict my food even more.

My weight plummeted to seven stone and my periods stopped completely. Even so, when I looked in the mirror all I saw was a fat, useless young mum. As I was so underweight, the fatigue just got worse as did my mood. Christopher did not sleep well at night, which added to my exhaustion. I would be pacing the floor with Christopher in my arms at 3 AM trying to get him to go back to sleep. Even worse, whenever Mary or my mum came to visit, they seemed to cope with Christopher so much better than I did. My self-worth was at an all-time low.

Shortly after we moved into our house, my friend Jackie came to visit me. She was so excited as she had just passed her driving test and was chattering on about her job. As a young mum who spent her day changing nappies, I felt like I had nothing in common with my friend anymore. After she left, I remember looking out the bedroom window and thinking, "Is this all there is to my life?" I was 19 years old and felt like an old woman. Suffering from postpartum depression affected the bonding process and my feelings towards Christopher were somewhat inconsistent. At times I would feel very loving and attentive towards him, but at other times I found myself reacting negatively or not responding to him at all. It didn't make me a bad person, I just didn't realise how ill I was. Unfortunately I kept these feelings to myself; on the few occasions that I tried talking to my mum about it, I felt that she wasn't listening or, even worse, that I was being judged. It wasn't her fault – in those days people didn't really know about postpartum depression.

When Christopher was born he weighed 9 pounds, 5 ounces, and was 21 inches long. Although some newborn babies can seem small and fragile, because of his size he was quite the little man. His skin was so smooth and creamy. He was beautiful. When he was about three months old, I remember people stopping me in the street and telling me what a beautiful boy he was. He had such a cute smile and was becoming quite a little charmer. Christopher often reacted to my changing moods. He wouldn't sleep and as a toddler he was quite defiant, but seemed to behave well with anyone else. At times I found myself disliking him, which made me hate myself even more. The guilt was overwhelming.

At eight months old he started to crawl. It was like a mini tornado had hit the house. He had suddenly found his freedom and would speed across the floor as fast as his chubby little knees could carry him, while giggling mischievously to himself. It was all a game to him and an open door was the perfect invitation for him to escape and explore. Con would often play with

Christopher (aged 2) ready for lunch

him, pretending to chase him and Christopher would squeal with delight. He would race across the room at a rate of knots until he was caught! Con would then swing him in the air and Christopher's chuckles could be heard all over the house. He had an infectious laugh and the smallest things seemed to amuse him.

The childproof gate at the bottom of the stairs was essential. Christopher could climb the stairs in seconds and I was so afraid he would fall. He loved to explore – I remember one morning when I was buried under a pile of ironing; I had given him some toys to play with on the floor, including a little wooden pull along dog which he called "Mim Mim." He would play with it for hours. Suddenly I realised that "Mim Mim" had been discarded and as I looked up from my ironing, I could see Christopher disappearing out of the dining room door like a bolt of lightning. I went after him to discover him in the lounge with a large pot of nappy cream which he had managed to open and was smearing himself with it. When I used to put the cream on

Christopher (aged 2) having fun in the bath

after I had changed his nappy, I would tell him that it was to make him smell nice. As he looked at me with a cheeky grin on his face all he kept saying to me was "mell, mell, mell." He was in a right mess. Sudocrem over his clothes and in his beautiful, golden-white hair. I quickly took the cream from him and told him that he was a naughty boy. He immediately screwed up his little face and started to cry. As I picked up my sticky little man and gave him a cuddle, I told him that he mustn't do that again because it was dangerous. Luckily he hadn't tried to eat it. Obviously now that he was crawling, I had to remember to put everything away.

When Christopher was two years old Con was sent to Wales to work on a six-month contract and only came home on the weekends. It was then that my mum stepped in.

"You can stay with me during the week while Con is away," she said.

It was a command, not an invitation. Con never complained. What I didn't know at the time was that it was her way of making sure I was eating properly. Ironically, she never actually confronted me about my weight because then we both would have had to admit I had a problem, but she knew it just the same. It must have hurt her to see how awful I looked. Getting back to eating normally was really tough. Mum did all the cooking and dished out my meals each evening. She was a great cook and her food was difficult to resist. The portions looked huge, but of course they were just normal size. The first evening I sat down to eat I picked up my knife and fork and stared at the food. Suddenly I felt famished. Mum glared at me, "What's wrong with it?" she said, proud of her cooking.

"Nothing, it's great," I said. I was scared of the consequences, but after months of starving myself, I ate it with relish.

The worst part was getting used to feeling full again. The desire to make myself sick was tremendous, but Mum was watching me like a hawk. Although I hated it, I was starting to put on weight and was feeling less depressed. I had also stopped making myself sick. I felt safe being back home with her and Dad – I sometimes wonder if my mum had actually saved my life. I wasn't completely cured but I know if I'd kept going, I could have ended up like Karen Carpenter, who was going through her own struggles with anorexia around the same time and eventually died from her disease. I now started to bond with Christopher and doing things for him was no longer a chore. I grew to love him even more. I still resent losing out on those first couple of years when I feel I should have been able to enjoy my son and show him the love he deserved, but I can't change it. I realise now it was because I had postpartum depression. I found going back home with Con on weekends hard, but when his contract came to an end, I moved back to our home permanently.

Putting on weight meant my periods restarted and even though they were somewhat irregular, in February I discovered I was pregnant again. This time it felt different. I was settling into married life and Christopher was going to have a little brother or sister.

When Christopher started school, it was obvious he was very bright. However, he would never settle in school and wouldn't do as he was told. In more recent times, he may have been considered to be on the autistic spectrum, but back in those days it wasn't recognised.

Although he was a bright boy, Chris did not do very well at school and struggled in mainstream education. He often didn't seem to see the point of what he was being taught. He would only make an effort if he found it meaningful. However, in his third year at primary school, he had a teacher who appeared to have a less academic approach to teaching. She encouraged the pupils in her class to explore their own interests and strengths. Ironically during that year he thrived and really seemed to enjoy school. He would meet me at the school gate full of what he had

Christopher (aged 2 and a half) and mummy having fun in the garden

done that day. According to EL Education (formerly Expeditionary Learning), "When students and teachers are engaged in work that is challenging, adventurous, and meaningful, learning and achievement flourish." On reflection I often wonder if he would have benefited from a more expeditionary learning educational model. He was such an inquisitive little boy. He was always asking questions about space or religion. He was such a deep thinker. One day he asked me quite a profound question.

"Mummy if I wasn't planned and Lizzie was, does that mean you love me less?"

I was quite shocked and desperate to reassure him. Who had he been listening or talking to?

"Of course it doesn't, I love you both the same," I said.

It broke my heart to think that he may have believed that. It bought back the guilt I felt about having postpartum depression and the impact it may have had on him. I just wanted him to know how much he was loved.

Chris was a great prankster. I used to go to a keep fit class every Thursday evening with my neighbour Christine. One evening in the summer of 1984 I got ready and went into the garden to let Con know I was leaving. Christine's two boys were in our garden playing and I could hear a lot of giggling. As I walked out of the back door Chris turned the garden hose on me and I got absolutely drenched. So there I was, dripping wet with an audience of four children and Con in fits of laughter. Needless to say, I had to dry off and change for my keep fit class.

As Christopher grew older his sense of humour developed even further. He loved doing impersonations, especially of people he knew, and was beginning to develop a real talent. He nicknamed my mum and dad "Jack" and "Vera" from *Coronation Street* and would mimic the way they spoke. He got their mannerisms to a tee. When my mum used to phone me, he would say: "Mum, Vera's on the phone," and then proceed to do an impersonation of her. She would pretend to get mad with him, but really she loved it. She idolised Christopher. Con's mum Mary has a very thick southern Irish accent; being half Irish himself, Christopher would pick up on some of the Irish phrases she would use and exaggerate them. It was like listening to a very young version of the comedian Dave Allen. I spoke to Christopher about joining a drama group, but he would just dismiss it as a bit of fun.

We shared the same sense of humour. We both loved slapstick comedy. One afternoon before Christmas, Christopher and I were the only ones at home. He was 12 or 13 at the time and the weather was miserable, so we decided to stay in to watch a 1970s comedy film that was just starting on TV called **Chase Me Comrade**, about a Russian ballet dancer defecting to the West during the Cold War. From the beginning of the film we were both in stitches and my sides were aching as I was laughing so much. I looked over at Christopher and he was crying with laughter. Halfway through, Con came home from work early and asked us what we were both laughing at. Christopher pointed to the TV, so Con sat down to watch it with us. The laughter in the room was so infectious Con was soon joining in. When the film had finished, Christopher turned to me and said, "I really enjoyed that, it was so funny."

It was a lovely afternoon spent with my son and I really felt so close to him that day.

Teenage turmoil
I remember coming home from shopping once when Christopher was about 14 and finding him and a friend, both drunk on Con's expensive Irish whiskey. He'd even topped the bottle up with water and put a wine cork in the top of the bottle

Christopher and Elizabeth in their teens spending an afternoon with Con

because he couldn't find the lid. I remember thinking it was just a teenage prank. Con reprimanded him when he came home from work but in private he treated it as a joke! I can't even say that I was turning a blind eye, I just didn't even think about it!

By the time he was 15, Christopher had changed from a funny, caring child into an angry young man with horrible mood swings. He had lost interest in school and I was constantly being asked to attend meetings about his behaviour and truancy. I was told by a number of his teachers that Christopher was exceptionally bright but he just wouldn't put the work in to achieve the grades he was capable of. He had totally lost any motivation to do well at school. He hated any form of authority. He would suddenly explode for no reason.

I remember him shouting at me because he believed the only reason I kept going to the school for meetings was because I fancied his head of year and not because I really cared about him. He would often demand money and when I refused to give it to him, he would get very aggressive. He would continuously shout at me and throw things around. Sometimes he would go out in the evenings and not come home. He was only 15. I would walk the streets at two in the morning looking for him. When he eventually came home, he told me he was with a friend all night and said I was overreacting. I put this down to puberty and ongoing problems at home.

Con and I were constantly arguing and at times it was like living in a war zone. Christopher was quick to put the blame on me because I was the one who wanted a divorce and in his words "trying to break up the family home." Indirectly, puberty may have been the cause, but what I didn't know was that Christopher was dabbling in drugs. I was so naive about drugs in those days, I didn't even consider he might be involved. I still don't know the extent of his drug taking but I do know that he was smoking cannabis and taking amphetamines (speed). Both of these drugs are associated with the onset of psychosis. Teenage tantrums are considered to be part of adolescence. Sometimes, however, I now know they can be a signal of something more serious.

After leaving school, Christopher started sixth form college in Maidstone, but after a couple months I got a letter saying he had been excluded from the course due to bad behaviour. He was getting into fights and not doing any of the course work. Following the same pattern as he did at school, I couldn't believe it. What made it worse was he seemed so ambivalent about it.

"I didn't like the course anyway," he said.

During this time he grew his hair long. Usually he kept it short and always had a trendy hair cut, but now it looked lank and unwashed. He had always bathed daily but he started to neglect his personal hygiene and he often had stains down his clothes. I tried to encourage him to change his clothes more regularly but it fell on deaf ears.

I can't deny that sometimes it was a relief when he went to stay with my parents for a few days as it gave me a break from his behaviour. Mum and Dad still seemed to have some positive influence over him, while Con and I were just wrapped up in what was going on with us.

In September 1993 my mum died of a stroke and Christopher, now 16, was devastated. He had become very close to her and would often go and stay with her and my dad when he found things too much at home. "Home" had become something of a battleground. Con and I were constantly arguing during that time and our marriage was clearly falling apart. It must have been awful for him. I sometimes wonder if things had been different if Mum hadn't passed away when she did. Despite her attitude towards me when she found out about my pregnancy, she absolutely doted on Christopher.

When Mum died, Christopher moved in with my dad. Initially it was for a few weeks to keep his granddad company, but then he decided to stay permanently. I was devastated. I pleaded with him to come home.

"Why should I come home with you and Dad when you are at each other's throats all the time? I'm much happier living with Granddad and he doesn't keep checking up on me all the time," he said.

He was 16 so I couldn't force him to come home. I had just started my second year at university and I think Christopher quite resented that. He was quite old fashioned in some ways. I remember him saying to me when he was at junior school, "Why can't you be 'old' like all of my friends' mums?" Bless him, I'm not sure what he meant by old, but I guess because I was much younger than most of the mothers at the school gate I tended to stand out. Of course he never knew how inadequate some of these women made me feel when I heard them talking about how wonderfully domesticated they were. I never felt that I fit in. No matter how much I try, I'm just not domesticated. I am an adequate cook at best but have always found housework to be a chore. Ironically one of the things Christopher did after he moved in with his granddad was enroll in a cookery course at the local adult education centre. He was a young man in a group of middle aged women, but that didn't seem to bother him. I think one of the ladies befriended him and helped him through the course. He took a real interest and soon became quite a good cook. I was so proud of him. It was so good to see him taking an interest in things again.

Chris loved to experiment with food. As a result, he also encouraged my dad to eat as his appetite had waned since Mum had passed away. His roast potatoes were amazing!

Although Christopher started to enjoy cooking, he didn't really see it as a career choice. He developed a keen interest in politics and, like my dad, he became a Labour Party supporter. This was when Margaret Thatcher was Prime Minister and unemployment had increased during her years in power. He did some research and found a residential college called Northern College in Barnsley that offered courses to people without any formal qualifications. He managed to secure a place there and enrolled on a one-year course that was a recognised pathway to university.

I remember the day I put him on the National Coach at the bus stop in Strood. I was feeling very emotional about him going so far away from home while at the same time being very excited for him. Things were looking up for him. He successfully completed the year by the skin of his teeth after a year of drinking and a relationship with a single mum, who I never met. I got the impression from him that there was no emotional attachment to her and that it was just sex! Other than that he never really spoke about her. He was offered a place at the North London University to study Politics and History and got accommodation in the halls of residence. He was following in my footsteps of a university education. Before leaving for university he got his hair cut and looked more like the old Christopher. I finally felt that Christopher was beginning to take control of his life and was looking to build a positive future for himself.

Christopher, Mary, and Con enjoying a laugh in the living room

Chapter 3
~
The Funeral

Both Christopher and Elizabeth were baptised into the Catholic Church as babies, but I always felt it was up to them to decide if they wanted to embrace the faith as they grew up. Elizabeth went to mass as a small child and took her first communion, but religion was never going to be part of her life. Christopher's faith was very strong as a young child, but he suddenly turned his back on the Catholic Church when he was about 11, flatly refusing to go to mass with Con, and I never really knew why. It broke Mary's heart. I suppose he was at an age when peer pressure began to be very strong and most of his friends weren't religious.

Perhaps I shouldn't have been surprised when he decided to return to the Church after he became ill in his early 20s. He never really spoke to me about the reasons why, but I respected his decision and supported him throughout. He started going for instruction classes and had a lovely sponsor who I later met during my involvement with the Church. Christopher was eventually confirmed into the Catholic Church and found great solace there. His faith remained absolute until he died and I knew he would want a Catholic funeral.

I felt overwhelmed thinking about Christopher's funeral and had no idea where to start or how to go about organising it. However, I was determined his funeral was not going to be morbid; I wanted it to be a celebration of his life. When I walked into the funeral director's office, I was so overwhelmed and didn't have a clue on how to proceed. Con still hadn't arrived back in the UK, but I needed to set the date. The assistant greeted me with kindness and understanding. I remember her telling me she had only intended to remain in the job for a year, but had stayed for 22 after she realised how important her job was to those who needed her. She spent a long time just listening to me, and when I cried she simply passed me a tissue. I felt her genuine compassion.

Elizabeth and I wanted a willow coffin instead of a traditional one. They are more eco-friendly and reminded me of a Moses basket for newborn babies. It felt like Christopher would be reborn. The funeral director then arranged the date for the funeral with the parish church. The following Saturday evening I had a call from Mary who said the parish priest had called her with his condolences. I can remember losing my temper and asked why he had contacted her and not me.

"I know I'm not Catholic, Mary, but I am Christopher's mother!" I wasn't angry with her, I was just feeling very raw.

"I don't know, dear," she said and I could hear the sadness in her voice. I felt like such a bitch.

An hour or so later the phone rang again.

"Is that Carol Ring?" The man who spoke had a very strong Irish accent.

"Yes, it is."

"It's Father Bill, parish priest from English Martyrs." Mary had obviously phoned him. "I am so sorry to hear about the death of your son. I knew him very well."

I found that very comforting.

"The mother is very important in the Catholic faith and

a mass is being said for Christopher tomorrow, so I would like to invite you to join me." I felt choked.

"Father, I'm not Catholic."

"I know, but that doesn't matter. The fact is you are Christopher's mother and I would love for you to come to mass tomorrow."

What could I say? It was a personal invitation. Amongst all the grief, I felt honoured to be asked. I know Christopher would have been so pleased.

"Thank you so much, I'll be there tomorrow."

The next morning, I decided to wear my black two-piece suit. It seemed appropriate to dress smartly. As I was driving to the church, I found myself talking to Christopher.

"I haven't felt so alone since you were born," I said and I could feel the tears welling up. Yet somehow it felt like Christopher was there with me.

I was one of the first to arrive at the church and I waited outside for a few minutes. When I went inside, the church felt huge and cold. I found a seat and looked around. It had been a long time since I'd been inside and as the worshippers began to arrive, I didn't recognise anyone. I started to question if I should be there, and that maybe I shouldn't have come. Then a lady I knew entered the church. She used to work at the TSB bank. She smiled and came and sat near me.

"How are you? I haven't seen you in ages." I tried to fight the tears but it was useless.

"My son died last Sunday. Father Bill phoned last night and invited me to mass."

She put her arm around me. "I'm so sorry," she said.

The church started to fill up but I still felt cold. I should have worn something warmer. Father Bill arrived and his presence seemed to fill the room. He was an older man with white hair and looked so majestic in his robes. I don't remember much about the mass until just before the end I heard my name called.

"Is Carol Ring here?" It was Father Bill. "Yes," I replied timidly.

He asked me to join him at the front of the church. As he held my hand he explained to the congregation about Christopher and who I was. He spoke about how everybody there were my new family and how they were there to support me. After the service had finished, many people came up to me and offered me such kind words. I will never forget it.

When Con finally arrived home, we agreed to meet at a local pub. Dad came with me and while he was up at the bar, Con walked in. He looked awful, a combination of grief and jet lag. He'd been told of Christopher's death over the phone by his sister-in-law. He had been a long way from home, alone, and with no family for support. As hard as it was for me, at least I had my family around me. When I spoke to him, he seemed dazed. Con was never one to express his feelings, but the pain was etched on his face. He told me to carry on making the funeral arrangements. I explained to him what I'd already done and asked if he wanted to make any changes.

"No," he said, "You're better at that stuff than me. I know it will be great." He told me not to worry about the cost, he would pay for it as he was earning good money in Kazakhstan. I had no savings and had been very worried about the financial aspect of the funeral. Con, bless him, saw the funeral as his responsibility.

It was another priest, Father Adrian, who helped me with the funeral arrangements. I never knew that he was fighting his own battle against cancer until after Christopher's funeral. This wonderful, brave man had been so supportive at the worst time in my life. I had never met him before Christopher's death and yet he gave me such comfort while facing his own struggles.

I had asked that people didn't wear black to the funeral. I wanted it to be a celebration of Christopher's life, I had even gone into Chatham to buy a new outfit. It felt bizarre shopping for my own son's funeral. A shop assistant came to ask if I needed any help. I could feel the tears welling up in my eyes.

"Are you ok?" she asked.

"I'm sorry, my son has died and I need an outfit for his funeral. I don't want to wear black, it feels so morbid. I want to celebrate his life."

"I'm so sorry," she said, "how old was he?"

"29," by this time I was crying. Unfazed, she showed me a light brown suit. Then I saw a bright red blouse and decided to wear them together. I still have the suit and blouse in my wardrobe, but I have never worn them again.

The morning before the funeral I had arranged for Christopher's coffin to lie open in the chapel of rest so people could pay their last respects. When I entered the chapel, Con and Mary were already there and Father Adrian was saying prayers. When he finished, I asked everyone to leave so I could have some time alone with my son. As I reached out to touch him, his body felt cold and lifeless. He wasn't there anymore, his body was just an empty shell. I told him how much I loved him and hoped that he was now at peace. When I left the room Father Adrian was waiting for me outside.

"Father, his body is so cold," I said.

"I know, it might help for you to think that Christopher's soul has left a mansion and is now in a beautiful palace." I took great comfort from that.

Chris and I often had a similar taste in music. As a child during the 1960s I loved the Beatles and my favourite was John

Lennon. In his teens he discovered the music of Lennon and loved the song "Imagine," the former Beatles' anthem of peace. It became his favourite song.

The night before Christopher's funeral there was a small service when his coffin was taken into the church. A few family and friends accompanied the coffin into the church while listening to John Lennon's "Imagine." I was feeling numb. I could hear voices behind me talking about how sad it was, but the words weren't really registering. All that was going through my mind was that Christopher was now at peace, he had been so unwell prior to his death. I think that is what got me through the early days of grief. Father Adrian told me that during one of their last meetings Christopher said he'd "had enough" and didn't want to go on any more. I didn't know how I was going to feel when I saw his face for the last time.

On the day of the funeral, the Church was packed to the rafters. So many people had come to say goodbye to Chris. Many of the younger people wore bright colours, but the traditionalists still wore black. My dad made a nod to both sides and wore a bright purple tie. I loved him for that. As I walked around the church to talk to people before the start of the service, a woman I'd never met before pressed a religious medal into my hand. She squeezed my hand so tightly while telling me what a lovely young man Christopher had been. She had known him through the church. It was such a kind and compassionate gesture.

A table at the front of the church was covered with mass cards and sympathy cards. In the Catholic Church people often send mass cards for the deceased, which means that a mass will be said for that person on a given date.

I wanted everyone to be included and had asked Father Bill if a blessing could be offered to the non-Catholics during the mass. Usually people who choose to have a blessing instead of communion were told to cross their arms across their chest as they approached the priest. I was surprised when he announced that only those who required blessing should go to him and that those who required communion should go to his assistant. He asked me up first and after the blessing, he hugged me.

During the service I spoke about Christopher and asked everyone to celebrate his life. I'd written down what I wanted to say and was determined to get through it myself. A friend had kindly volunteered to finish it for me if I broke down, but I felt I owed it to Christopher to do this for him. I spoke about Christopher's achievements and how I wanted everyone to remember him. It was, and still is, important to me that Christopher is not forgotten. My dad was so proud that I managed to get through it.

The worst part of the funeral for me was when the coffin was lowered into the grave. I remember turning around to search for Elizabeth. I saw her two friends, Nicole and Kelly, standing on either side of her. She looked so distraught, it was almost like they were physically holding her up. I was so grateful to those two girls that day for looking after my daughter so well. She had met Nicole at school and Kelly was Nicole's big sister. They are still very good friends. Then, my friend Tracy came up to me. She told me that Christopher was now at peace and his demons were no more and gave me a massive hug. Tracy was a long standing friend. I first met Tracy and her partner when she worked in my local cafe. She had told me about her own issues with mental health and how they affected her life on a daily basis. She had often spoken to Christopher when he came to the cafe with me. She understood what he was going through and had become a good friend. On the card she sent she had written: "Chris, no more demons." Christopher's key worker Kumar also came to the funeral and was visibly very upset. He kept saying he wished he had done more for Christopher, but I tried to reassure him that he had done as much as he could and shouldn't feel in any way bad at all.

I had arranged the wake at the Coach & Horses. It was the family's local pub and everyone knew Christopher. The pub was packed with family and friends from several generations wanting to express their condolences and to celebrate his life. To be honest, it all felt quite surreal. The sun was shining and I was sitting in the pub garden with Dad, Elizabeth, Sue, Con, and Con's girlfriend. I didn't want the day to end because that meant I would have to finally let Christopher go. That night I cried myself to sleep. During the wake we all had a photo taken (Sue, me, Kelly, Elizabeth, Tracy, and Nicole). It was almost like a pact we had that Christopher would always remain in our hearts.

Chapter 4

~

Psychosis

I started to notice a change in Christopher during his first year at university, in his early 20s. One day when he was home for a weekend visit and staying with his dad, I received a worried phone call from Elizabeth.

"Mum, Chris is acting really strangely," she said. "He keeps looking out from behind the curtains and saying people are out to get him. He's scaring me."

"Ok, I'll come round," I said. By now Con and I had put our differences aside and I knew he wouldn't mind.

When I saw Christopher, his eyes seemed very vacant.

"Mum," he said, "I think I would be better off living on the streets. I don't deserve to live here."

"Don't be silly Chris. Why are you talking like that?" Then something occurred to me. "Are you hearing voices?" I asked. I didn't really believe that he was hearing voices. It was really a tongue in cheek remark as I was so taken aback by what he said. Why would he say something like that? I thought he was joking.

"No," he replied. But I was still worried. He looked dishevelled and appeared so distant. In the past he had always paid attention to his personal hygiene.

According to the Mental Health Foundation (2021) hearing voices doesn't necessarily mean that you are mentally unwell. One in 10 people may experience this at some time in their lives. It may be related to a traumatic life event or stress. It can also be caused by lack of sleep or extreme hunger. It can be the side effects of recreational or prescribed drugs. However, if you or a member of your family are hearing voices it's advisable to see your doctor to discuss the possible cause.

A week after Christopher went back to university, I received an odd phone call from him. He wasn't making sense and repeatedly said that monks were coming into his room at night and touching him. He also spoke about Mary, the Virgin Mother, being there with him and telling him he was a bad person and needed to be punished. I persuaded him to come home and took him to a GP doctor, though the doctor wasn't particularly helpful and didn't like that I came into the consultation with Christopher. Christopher in turn wasn't honest about what was happening to him and, as a result, he was sent away with a prescription for antidepressants. I was furious, but didn't see what else I could do.

One day I was at my dad's when Christopher told me he was going to take a CD of the Beatles back to the shop as he was hearing strange voices on some of the tracks. Later when he came back with a replacement he said the same thing was happening with the new one. I didn't take too much notice at the time, but in hindsight I now believe he was hearing voices.

Christopher returned to university, which proved to be a very successful first year for him academically and he came home for the summer. I don't really remember the chronology of events after that, but I do remember when he came home. Christopher became worse. At that time I was working for the

Eating Disorder Service in Maidstone. I was so worried about Chris I spoke to our consultant psychiatrist about Chris. I explained about the GP's attitude and that I felt he hadn't taken my concerns seriously.

She advised me to telephone the surgery and tell them that I had spoken to her about my anxieties and Chris needed to be seen urgently. Subsequently I was offered an appointment that evening. When I took Chris to see the GP, his attitude was entirely different. I informed him about the changes in Chris's behaviour and that he was seeing things that others couldn't see. As a result the doctor made an urgent referral to the CMHT. I felt a bit resentful that I had to get my consultant psychiatrist involved in order for my concerns to be taken seriously, but at least Chris was finally getting the help he needed.

Christopher was eventually taken on by the local CMHT who prescribed him antipsychotics. He went back to university for the 2000 Autumn term, but when he came home for Christmas break, the change in him was too great to ignore; he was almost unrecognisable. He had neglected himself and had lost a great deal of weight. It was clear that he wasn't washing, his hair was unkempt, and he hadn't shaved for weeks. He was seen by his community mental health nurse who recommended an increase in his medication. I hoped that this would help, but three days before Christmas I was returning from work on the train from London when my dad phoned me and destroyed any hope that my son was improving.

"Carol," he said, "Chris has admitted himself to hospital. He can't cope anymore."

I got to the hospital and was told that Christopher had been admitted to the psychiatric unit. I spoke to the nurse who said I could see Christopher, but he had been heavily sedated. True enough, he was like a zombie and didn't even seem to recognise me. It was awful. How could my baby have come to this? I started crying to the male nurse who could see how distressed I was.

"Chris is very ill right now and he needs relief from his symptoms," he said. "That's why we've sedated him. I promise we'll look after him."

I left the hospital that night with a broken heart.

On Christmas Day I got up early and Mitch found me sobbing in the lounge. He hugged me and told me, "Chris is going to be ok. Let's get dressed and go to the hospital."

Con's parents, my dad, Con, Elizabeth, Mitch, and I arrived at the hospital all armed with presents just as the staff were laying the table for Christmas lunch. I remember one of the other patients telling me he was Father Christmas and asking me to sit on his knee.

"Come on, I need to know what you want for Christmas," he said. A bit of humour was just what we needed.

Christopher asked if he could come home, but was told by the nurse that he needed to stay in the hospital. He was less sedated and therefore more aware of his surroundings. We stayed for a couple of hours and were advised by staff to take Christopher's presents home. The only one he insisted on keeping was the silver crucifix which I had bought him.

Three months later Christopher was considered well enough to come home and was discharged on antipsychotic medication. He had been diagnosed with psychotic depression (major depression that includes psychotic features) and I was hoping his illness was a one-off episode, as happens occasionally. His treatment appeared to have been successful.

Unfortunately at that time I wasn't aware that one of the side effects of taking olanzapine is weight gain, as it stimulates the appetite. Christopher became quite obese which can seriously affect your health. These days people who are taking antipsychotic medication have regular physical health checks and are given dietary advice. However, this didn't happen when Christopher was under the mental health services.

Christopher went back to university and I hoped he would be able to put the experience behind him. Unfortunately he soon decided to stop taking his medication, saying he didn't need it anymore. Inevitably, it wasn't long before his psychotic symptoms started to reoccur. When I went to bring him home, I found he had been isolating himself at university and not mixing with his flatmates. He was spending all his time in his room alone. The room was a complete mess and he had no sheets on the bed. As I packed up all of his belongings and took him to the car, my heart was breaking. I just couldn't believe this was happening to my son. I just didn't know how to help him. The early Intervention Psychosis Team that I work for recognised the impact of this illness on families and now employs carer peer support workers who have lived experience of caring for a loved one with psychosis to work with families. I would really have appreciated this support if it had been available in the 90s.

His delusions were, once again, religious in nature and he was experiencing hallucinations. He was becoming paranoid and now believed he was a bad person who deserved to be punished. He described seeing monks, dressed in traditional habits, who would tell him he was a bad person and now and again he would even feel them touching him. He was very withdrawn and flat in mood. Once again he had neglected his self-care and looked unkempt. He had also lost more weight. I was very worried and spoke to his community mental health nurse. She managed to get him an emergency appointment with the community consultant psychiatrist who spoke to Christopher about his non-compliance with the antipsychotic drugs and how this had led to him becoming unwell again. He reluctantly agreed to start taking the medication again and gradually his symptoms started to reduce.

After his relapse, Christopher decided to return to university and finish his degree. Reluctantly he agreed for me to accompany him to a meeting with his personal tutor. During the meeting the tutor appeared surprised that Christopher had been so ill.

"I would never have known," he said. "He did a presentation in front of his group last term of a very high standard."

Apparently Christopher had been performing very well in his studies that year, and was on course for a first-class degree. His tutor was certainly keen to support him in whatever way he could. As a result, Christopher was given a computer and additional IT support. He was also given a mentor who he could talk to whenever he felt stressed. She set up regular meetings with Christopher. It was agreed that Christopher would still live at home and travel to London daily as he had found living in student accommodation too stressful. I started to feel very positive about Christopher's future. However, despite the additional support, he was not able to complete his second year. He started to become paranoid of his mentor.

Dealing with Christopher's mental health problems often felt like the film *Groundhog Day*. Situations would repeat themselves again and again. The major issue was that he lacked insight into his illness, that is, he didn't have any awareness that he was in fact ill, and that he could become better by taking his antipsychotic medication. Not only was schizophrenia his reality, it was the way the world was and nothing could change that. As a result, he would periodically rebel: refusing to attend appointments with his mental health team or refusing his medication. This would quickly lead to a relapse. Christmas seemed to be a prime time for these relapses. One year I was staying with my dad and was woken at 2 AM to Christopher chanting the rosary. After about an hour of listening to this I went into his room to find him sitting up on his bed staring into space with blue rosary beads in his hands.

"Chris, what are you doing?" I said.

"Saying the rosary," he calmly replied.

"Chris, you need to stop now and go to sleep." But he didn't seem to hear me and the chanting continued all night.

Mitch had gone to visit his daughter for Christmas so it was only Dad, Christopher, and me for Christmas lunch, as Elizabeth was working at Battersea Dogs Home. While I was cooking lunch, Christopher seemed very agitated. He kept pacing and refused anything to eat or drink. My heart sank and I knew he was relapsing. This was happening quite frequently and was fast becoming a normal way of life for us as a family. I laid the table and dished up the dinner. Christopher picked at his food and then said he was going back to bed. My dad sighed.

"Not again," he said. "I can't cope with this anymore."

"Dad, I think we should speak to the mental health services about some sort of supported housing," I said.

"He won't go," Dad replied.

"Dad, he may have no choice. He can't cope on his own and we won't always be here to help him. I want him to be able to live independently. Being in supported housing will help him."

It was clear we were heading for another hospital spell.

Mary had invited us all to lunch on Boxing Day. Con was there so I had a chance to speak to him about Christopher.

"Con, Dad and I had an awful day with Chris yesterday. He's becoming unwell again," I said.

"Not taking his tablets again, you mean?"

I could hear the exasperation in his voice. The frustrating thing was that all the time Christopher complied with his treatment he remained relatively well. The problem was his lack of insight.

Christopher left Mary's after a couple of hours saying he was going home to sleep. Then about half an hour later he walked past the house with cans of Guinness that he got from the local shop. When Dad and I got home, the place smelled of vomit. Christopher had drunk all the Guinness and had been sick in the lounge and kitchen. Dad was furious. I went upstairs to find Christopher unconscious on the bed, having drunk himself into a stupor, apparently to get relief from his symptoms.

For the rest of the Christmas period, I tried to keep him safe until the CMHT were back at work as he refused to go to hospital. I managed to get him an emergency appointment but he refused to go. Dad was at his wits end, "I don't think I can have him living here," he said, "I can't cope with him like this."

Eventually I managed to persuade Christopher to go see the doctors. They spent all day trying to get him to go into hospital on a voluntary basis so he could be assessed, but Christopher adamantly refused.

"Can't you section him?" I asked. How much worse did he have to get?

"He's not quite at the stage where I can section him," but in another week he probably will be," the doctor explained. "He needs to go back on his medication now."

I heard a raised, angry voice. It was Con.

"Why don't you just take the bloody medication and we can all go home!"

"Is that all I need to do?" Christopher said in a small voice. "Will they let me go home then?"

"Yes."

"Ok, I'll take them."

I was gobsmacked. Con's approach had worked. Christopher had become a little boy being told off by his dad. I phoned my dad to see if he would have him back.

"I'll have him in the house if he allows me to give him the tablets so that I know he's taking them."

Christopher agreed to this. He loved living with his granddad as he felt safe there. Finally we had reached a compromise, of sorts.

But soon Christopher started seeing things again and became increasingly paranoid. It was a pattern he continued to follow, going from one psychotic episode to another. Eventually he was diagnosed with schizophrenia. He struggled with basic life skills and daily living and was finally offered a place at Pathways, which was supported housing for people with mental health problems. It was a stepping-stone to independent living, but to be honest Christopher wasn't ready for this. He found being away from his grandfather very difficult as he had always felt safe there. Despite lots of encouragement and support from the staff at Pathways, it proved too much for him and he was soon back living with my dad.

Christopher felt very threatened by my role as a mental health nurse and accused me of colluding with the mental health services against him, when in fact all I was doing was trying to keep my son safe. I loved my son, but inside my heart was breaking as I felt helpless.

At the time I was working as a specialist eating disorder nurse and was very naive about psychosis. Most of my knowledge about its treatment was from textbooks during my nurse training. I don't remember talking to Christopher about any side effects he was experiencing from the antipsychotics, or if he was finding them troublesome. All I wanted was for him to be safe and symptom free. I didn't look beyond the medication.

What I did know was that Christopher's self-esteem was rock bottom. He hated the way he looked due to the weight gain. I know he would have loved to have been in a relationship, but believed that no one would want him because of the way he looked. Today I would expect him to be offered psychological therapy and social support, but back then I (or we) didn't use these methods. He would have also seen a physical health nurse who would have helped him with his weight gain. Many of the newer antipsychotics prescribed today don't cause weight gain.

Christopher went back to the Catholic Church and seemed to find great solace there. I know that the priests at English Martyrs in Strood showed my son great kindness and love, but Christopher was growing weary and confided in one of the priests that he no longer wanted to live. He was tired of constantly fighting his demons. For peace, he drank until he blacked out so the demons, or anyone else, couldn't reach him.

Unsurprisingly, Christopher's lack of insight led to an increased number of relapses. He disengaged with the mental health services and began to isolate himself. His hands were full of bruises from when he punched the wall in anger. When, once again, he didn't turn up for an appointment, his Community Psychiatric Nurse (CPN) phoned me to ask how Christopher was. I told her my concerns and she decided to make an unannounced visit and asked if Con and I could go with her. I phoned my dad and let him know that we were coming, but not to tell Christopher. When we got there my dad answered the door and Christopher was standing behind him. He glared at me and raised his fist at me. "You fucking bitch," he said. But his CPN stood up for me, "Don't have a go at your mum. It was my idea to come and see you."

Had Christopher lived, I have to question whether his life would have been a case of endless relapses and hospital admissions. Would I really want that for him? Deep down, I know the answer is no. It was a constant battle just to get him to comply with his treatment. Would he have ever responded to treatment, including therapy? The illness robbed him of his identity; his heart and soul were slowly being eaten away. Today I grieve more for Christopher's life than for his death. Towards the end of his life the monsters in his head were so powerful. I had become the enemy who colluded with the mental health services to keep him trapped. I miss my vibrant, inquisitive little boy who used to make me laugh with his impressions and jokes.

The night Christopher passed away I knew he was finally at peace. His demons were gone. He was leaving a very dark place and moving towards light. Thanks to my faith, I believe Christopher is now in the arms of angels who are taking good care of him.

Many people with mental health problems have great insight into their condition and learn to manage their lives really well. I am not sure whether Christopher would ever have been able to achieve that. His lack of insight always held him back from making any real improvements to his life. That's not to say that he hadn't achieved anything in his short life. Before schizophrenia had taken hold, he had become an amazing cook. He had gone to college and had completed the first year of his university degree with flying colours.

The fact that he didn't believe he was ill created a lot of conflict between Christopher and me. He would refuse to take his treatment because he didn't think there was anything wrong with him. He would accuse me of colluding with his mental health nurse. I got very frustrated with him and felt he was just being stubborn. Trying to convince him that the medication would make him better was impossible. This would then lead to another relapse, which became more frequent.

I recently came across the term anosognosia, which refers to when a person is unaware they have a disability. It can affect up to 50% of people with schizophrenia. It is one of the main reasons why they don't comply with treatment. Anosognosia in people with schizophrenia is associated with treatment adherence and the frequency of relapse which can result in coercive treatment and hospitalisation.

I believe this could have applied to Christopher.

Chapter 5

~

The First Six Months

The first six months after Christopher's death were surreal. Not only was I learning to cope with the loss of my son, but my long-term relationship with Mitch had also come to an end. My life felt like it had completely fallen apart.

Relationships

They say losing a child often leads to the breakup of your relationship. In fact, a survey by Compassionate Friends in 2006 concluded that divorces among bereaved parents are more common than most people think. I felt so hurt and abandoned by Mitch when he left me following Christopher's death. He left me at a time when I needed him most and it's not something I can ever forgive him for. I had always been there for him and took good care of him following his stroke and again when he had prostate cancer. How could I have stayed with such a self obsessed man for so long?

Even though Mitch had been Chris's stepfather for 13 years, he seemed to lack any empathy with the pain I was suffering, and, as a result, I couldn't turn to him for support. To be honest, our relationship was already in crisis. I had moved out two months before Chris's death and was in the process of buying my own home, but until then neither of us had been able to make the final break. Christopher's passing was the final nail in the coffin of our relationship. We no longer had anything in common and continuing the relationship was destroying us both. I needed all my emotional energy to cope with Christopher's death, and finally admitted the relationship had run its course.

I know Mitch had his own theory about why our relationship ended, but unfortunately he made accusations that had no real foundation. The final year we were together I had been extremely miserable. I had broken my leg earlier in the year, which had delayed my moving out. I knew he was constantly checking my mobile and he accused me of having an affair with a work colleague.

Even though I was doing nothing wrong, I began deleting texts after I had read them and kept my phone on silent so I wouldn't have to explain myself after every call. Unfortunately, to Mitch this was more proof of my guilt, and he would phone me when we were together, as if having my phone on silent demonstrated my infidelity! Mitch could not understand how I could be friends with a male work colleague and there be nothing more than friendship.

I found this particularly difficult to deal with, especially as I knew Mitch had been discussing my "affair" with our friends and his own children. I guess his kids felt they should be loyal to their father and became very distant towards me, no longer replying to my texts or voicemails. Fortunately, our mutual friends chose not to take sides and are still in touch today. However, I went through a stage of not knowing who to trust and found myself becoming very guarded. I remember Michael, my sympathetic colleague, coming into my office after Mitch and I had finally split up and asked, "Can we be friends again now?" He had also been deeply hurt by Mitch's accusations. It was a no brainer, "Of course we can," I said. Once again, I felt free to choose my own friends, whether male or female.

After we split up, Mitch still spent a lot of time with my friends Sue and Malc, which I resented. Sue had originally been my friend and I had known her for a long time. As the years had passed, we had all become close friends and we regularly went out as a foursome. Consequently, I knew I didn't have the right to ask Sue to choose between us, so I kept my distance and inadvertently distanced myself from her in the process.

One weekend I walked into the local café where the four of us had regularly met for Saturday morning breakfast, in order to meet some other friends. As I walked in, I saw Sue and Malc having breakfast with Mitch. I ran out of the café in a flood of tears and drove into Strood, from where I sent Mitch a vile text. I can't remember what exactly I said but I think I may have wished him dead. I didn't really mean it, but I was so hurt and angry.

Sue later told me later that Mitch had led her to believe that I would be there when he had asked them to join him. We had thought we may be able to remain "friends," but, to be honest, I couldn't. I am saddened that my friends got caught up in the unpleasantness of our breakup. Although I can't take words back, I apologise unreservedly to anyone who may have been hurt by things I said back then. I was angry. I was vulnerable. I couldn't understand, and I still can't understand, why Mitch was being so thoughtless at a time when I needed support the most.

Returning to work

I went back to work four days after Chris's funeral. My decision had, in part, been driven by an invitation I received from a young person at the school where I worked. At the time I had been working as a CPN based in a secondary school and had supported a sixth form student who had subsequently been nominated for a young person's award. The ceremony was at the Winter Gardens in Margate. My student could bring along her parents plus two other guests. I was honoured that she chose me and one of the school counsellors to accompany her, because we had helped her so much. In a strange way I knew Christopher would have wanted me to go. The ceremony was on the Sunday evening before I was due to go back to work. It felt very strange and I was in a bit of a daze, but I was determined to go.

The school counsellor and I travelled down together by train. It was a bittersweet irony that both her son and her husband had been killed in a road accident twenty years earlier. She was so supportive that night. Our young person didn't win the award, but her determination and progress, despite her difficulties, were greatly acknowledged. I was so proud of her as she stood on the stage. A while later, another young woman was called onto the stage. I barely remember her introduction but what I do remember was her beautiful singing voice. As she began singing Eva Cassidy's version of "Somewhere Over The Rainbow," the room fell silent. I was mesmerised. It wasn't perfect, but the wrong notes didn't detract from her wonderful performance. So many young people were recognised for their achievements that night. On the train journey home, I thought about all that Christopher had achieved in his short life despite the obstacles he had faced. The young woman who sang that night would never know what an inspiration she had been to me.

The day after the awards ceremony I went back to work as planned. It helped that I enjoyed my job working with young people. A friend of mine asked how I had made it through those early dark days after Christopher died. I told her I didn't know, I just did because I had to. I managed to continue working with the support of my lovely manager Ruth. She agreed I could start later and finish earlier which meant I would be there during school hours to see the young people I was supporting, and that was really all that mattered to me.

Most of the staff were very supportive and understanding. Although one member of the pastoral staff was quite spiteful, talking loudly about some staff not pulling their weight when I was in the room. I didn't have the energy to confront her, but I remember thinking how I hoped she would never have to experience losing a child. I felt quite sorry for her really, compassion costs nothing. My manager soon got wind of her behaviour and put a stop to it.

Another member of staff with whom I had always gotten on well was walking towards me down the classroom corridor, I saw the look of horror on her face as she darted into one of the classrooms. I felt so hurt and mentioned the episode to one of the other nurses. The next time I saw her she came running up to me and put her arms around me and said, "I'm so sorry I just didn't know what to say."

The first few months after Chris passed away, I seemed to hit the self-destruct button. I was overwhelmed by anger and guilt. I blamed myself for his illness and ultimately for his death. Newly single, I felt very lonely and tried hard not to burden Elizabeth and my dad with my despair.

Every night after work I would stop at the local Co-op and buy a ready made meal and wine. Then I would retreat into the world of soap operas, starting with *Hollyoaks* and ending with *Coronation Street*, until Elizabeth came home from work. I would spend a bit of time with her and then go to bed. I found it impossible to sleep and drank copious amounts of wine while watching quiz shows on night-time TV. I would eventually fall asleep about 3 AM. Sometimes it was all I could do to keep sane. I had no partner or husband to talk to. The loneliness was unbearable.

One night I was feeling very depressed. Everything seemed to come to a head. I was laying in bed watching a quiz programme and had drunk wine until 3 AM. I just wanted to feel nothing and the alcohol wasn't helping. I found some painkillers in my handbag and took half a dozen with a huge mouthful of wine. Then I laid on my pillow and waited for it to take effect. All it did was knock me out for a few hours, and when I came to I felt so ashamed. My poor Elizabeth, what was I thinking?! How could I even think about leaving her and Dad after what they were already going through. I suddenly remembered that I had a doctor's appointment that morning. I don't know how I managed to drive the short journey to the surgery and when I sat in front of my doctor she looked at me and asked, "Have you been drinking?"

I burst into tears.

"I'm so sorry," I cried, "I feel so depressed. Why did Christopher have to die?"

I didn't tell her about the tablets. "Carol, what can I do to help?"

"Give me my son back," I said.

"I can't do that," she said kindly. "If you hadn't been drinking, I would send you to the hospital for a mental health assessment."

It was a sudden wake up call. "I'll be ok."

"Are you sure?"

"Yes," I reassured her. "I'll be ok."

This wasn't the way to deal with losing Christopher.

A few days later I had a call from my doctor. Apparently, she had been so worried about me that she phoned to see if I was ok. I reassured her that I was feeling better and found myself apologising for going to her surgery in such a state. She was so understanding and gave the details of the group Compassionate

Friends, who offer many kinds of support for bereaved parents, including a telephone helpline to contact for support.

I have a photo of Christopher taken in the year before he died on display on the sideboard in my dining room. Sometimes when I look at it, I want to pull him out of it and would give anything for him to be alive again. Although it has gotten easier, I am still on a journey and some days can feel really brutal. I'm going to be honest and say that suicidal thoughts often came into my mind, it wasn't just the once. At least I wouldn't have to cope with the pain any more. I was finding these feelings quite scary, especially as I had already made one pseudo attempt and what if next time I really meant it? One morning I phoned the Compassionate Friends helpline and spoke to one of the volunteers. When I told her how I was feeling, she said, "I haven't spoken to one bereaved parent who hasn't felt suicidal at some time. What you are feeling is perfectly normal after losing a child."

She was so kind and reassuring.

"You can phone us at any time. Don't feel that you have to cope on your own. The helpline is manned by other bereaved parents who know what you are going through."

At least now I knew that there was someone on the end of the phone who would understand if I needed to talk. Of course, these days there are many active groups on social media that can be very supportive at a time like this.

Family

After Christopher died, I found myself clinging to my dad for comfort. He made me feel safe. Dad had developed quite a social life at the local pub he went to and so I started to join him there. Twice a week he would meet his friend for an afternoon drink and a natter, so after work I would meet them both and have a glass of wine and a packet of crisps, then I would give Dad a lift home. It gave me something to look forward to.

I always had a special bond with my dad and this strengthened in the months after Christopher passed away. I was always at his house and the Coach & Horses became my second home. I couldn't have coped so well in the early days without him. He had been like a second father to Christopher and his grief was as raw as mine. I was on my own and had no partner to rely on. We didn't spend lots of time talking about Christopher, but it was reassuring being with him as I didn't want to burden Elizabeth as she was dealing with her own grief. I became very paranoid about her coming to harm and would constantly phone her when she came home late from work. Although all she was doing was socialising with friends from Battersea Dogs Home, I couldn't bear the thought of losing her, too. Lots of bereaved parents become fearful of losing their other children, which is a fairly common reaction.

One day I had a phone call from Elizabeth.

"Mum, I'm going to foster a beaten up old Staffie. He hates being in kennels and is really distressed."

"Elizabeth, I really don't think it's a good idea." I replied, with apprehension.

"Mum, he will be fine," Elizabeth reassured me.

"What about the cats?" I asked.

"He's been cat tested. He is fine with cats."

I wasn't convinced, but I agreed. That night the front door opened and in walked "Arthur Bear" with his lead in his mouth and I immediately fell in love with him. He was elderly and had health issues so was unlikely to be re-homed. Elizabeth decided to adopt him and he came to live with us permanently. He was such an adorable dog and gave us something to focus on. He went to work with Elizabeth every day and every evening when they came home I started playing fetch the ball with him. If I didn't play for some reason then he would stand in front of me and bark until I got the ball! I really loved the old boy. He was such good company, especially when Elizabeth went out in the evenings and I was on my own. Arthur always slept in Elizabeth's room with her so if she was staying out overnight I would get into Elizabeth's bed and Arthur would lay beside me, quietly snoring. I didn't feel quite so alone. Sometimes on Elizabeth's day off she would join us at the pub and bring Arthur. Everyone loved him. Everyone began to know who Arthur was and he was always made a big fuss over.

Even as a young child, Elizabeth was so caring and sharing. When Elizabeth was three years old, I bought her a cuddly, soft toy dog for Christmas that she called Max. She treasured him and took him to bed every night, refusing to sleep if he wasn't there. Whenever she stayed at her grandparent's or friend's he always had to go with her. One night after Christopher died, when Elizabeth came home from work, I was laying on my bed sobbing. She never said anything but a few minutes later I felt Elizabeth put something gently on the bed. When I looked up, she had left my room and I saw she had given me her beloved Max to help comfort me. She still had him. It was such a lovely, kind gesture. I was so full of emotion and held Max very tightly while I cried myself to sleep.

Christmas and Socials

Christmas of 2006 was awful. Mitch invited me and my dad for Christmas day and I decided to accept his invitation. I was confused and didn't really know what to do. Elizabeth was working and it was my first Christmas without Christopher. At least it was familiar but it proved to be a terrible mistake. The atmosphere was horrible and all we did was argue. My poor dad got angry and wanted to go home but I couldn't get him a taxi. Luckily Elizabeth popped in after work to get her present and gave us both a lift. I was glad to get back home and have a couple of Christmas drinks with my daughter before going to bed. Just after that was when I decided to cut all ties with Mitch. It wasn't working trying to stay friends.

At times it felt like I had two dads. I would sit at the bar in between Dad and his friend Brian drinking my one glass of wine and a packet of crisps while we put the world to rights. We were like the three amigos. One afternoon when I was having a drink with my Dad, Brian mentioned that the darts player Bobby George was playing an exhibition match at another local pub called the Cecil Arms. So, after I dropped Dad off home, I joined Brian to watch the exhibition. The atmosphere in the pub was brilliant. I thought how Christopher would have loved to have been there to watch it.

Bobby proved to be a real showman. I remember how he invited an eager young man with Down Syndrome to play against him and let him win. The smile on the young man's face was priceless.

Elizabeth was also there with a few friends. I was getting a bit loud after a few glasses of wine and I think she got a bit embarrassed. I heard one of her friends tell her, "Leave your Mum alone, she is enjoying herself." However, I became a little self-conscious and quietened down a bit. Bless him, Brian was well away and hardly noticed.

In February 2007 Brian asked me if I would give him a lift to a working man's club in Gillingham that was hosting a Swing and Jazz night as he had been drinking and would have been over the drink drive limit. He used to play the drums when he was younger and although he was now in his 70s he still had a passion for music.

"You can come if you like. I know the band and they will let you in."

Although in reality he needed a lift, I was chuffed to be asked as I love Swing music. So, in exchange for a free night out and a pint of cider shandy, I agreed to be chauffeur for the evening. It was a wonderful distraction and for a few hours I was able to forget my pain. The music was amazing and was a great tribute to the Rat Pack Singers Frank Sinatra, Dean Martin, and Sammy Davis Junior.

I don't see my cousin Christine very often, but one Sunday morning a couple of months after Christopher's death I found myself parked outside a shop a few doors away from where she lives, in floods of tears. I remember walking up to her house and knocking on the front door. When she opened the door, she didn't ask any questions, she asked me in and promptly sat me down. "Cup of tea?" she said. Christine was so good to me that day. She just let me talk and cry until I was exhausted. Then her husband Les gave me a large glass of red wine and made me laugh as only he can. Thanks guys, it's what I really needed that day. Christine and I do still keep in touch but it's mainly by text and social media. I feel so fortunate to have had the support of these people in my life at that time. It helped me get through such a dark time.

Christopher's Journal

A few days after Christopher died, Elizabeth and I were going through his things when we came across his journal. One of things that struck me was that it was written in pencil in an exercise book. It felt quite childlike, and as I began reading it I felt like an intruder. He wrote about how mental health services were controlling his life and how he wasn't free. He referred to me as a "social worker" who was in collusion with them. It was the same as a conversation I often had with him, especially when his review meeting was due, or he needed his injection. He had never fully engaged with the CMHT and even when he was symptom-free, he still believed what he experienced in his psychotic episodes were real. Many of Christopher's delusions were religious in nature. He believed he was a bad person and was being punished by God. Even the Catholic priests at the English Martyrs Church in Strood could not convince him God wouldn't be so cruel as to treat him that way. I remember sitting with him and Father John at the priest's house the year before. For over two hours Father John tried unsuccessfully to convince Christopher that God loved him, and his auditory and visual hallucinations were not real. Although Christopher's faith was absolute and he had complete respect for the priests, they were unable to rid him of his fixed delusions. The reality was that Christopher was very ill and needed the support of the CMHT. At times when he became a danger to himself, I needed to intervene and alert them that he was relapsing. I can understand why he would see me as colluding with them, when all I was doing was trying to keep him safe.

Anniversaries

In October 2007, Christopher would have been 30. The first birthday after he passed away would have been difficult enough, but this would have been a milestone. I wanted to mark the day and decided I would have a 30th birthday party for him at our local pub. On my friend Tracy's advice, I took the day off work and went to his grave with a friend. We sat by his gravestone and raised a glass of wine to his memory. After I collected my dad, we went to the pub. I had only invited a few special friends to the party, but I was pleased Con was home and able to come. The emotion of the day was overwhelming. I got very drunk and

Elizabeth had to take me home and put me to bed. As well as the party in the Coach & Horses, I organised a Sunday birthday lunch for Christopher's birthday at a local restaurant. Mitch refused to come, which hurt me deeply. A mutual friend told me he felt it was disrespectful. Con had to go back to work abroad and I don't remember seeing much of him in those early days, but I'm sure being alone with his own grief in a foreign country couldn't have been easy for him. He is now back in the UK and I am in regular contact with him. I know I can always talk to him about our son.

Chapter 6
~
Green Shoots and Black Clouds

When a friend suggested I join an online dating site I thought, "Why not?"

When I mentioned it to Elizabeth, she was horrified. Online dating wasn't as socially acceptable then as it is today and she was concerned for my safety. Eventually, when she realised I was serious, she helped me set up my profile and insisted she should be able to keep an eye on it. Talk about role reversal!

The first couple of dates I went on were fairly disastrous, but I was sensible enough to ensure I was safe. When it became clear that one guy only had one thing on his mind, I phoned Elizabeth to come and get me. She wasn't pleased and started to lecture me about the dangers of online dating.

"I've already lost my brother and I don't want to lose you too," she scolded.

After that experience I decided to call it a day. But when I logged in to delete my profile, I saw someone had left a message for me. It was very brief, simply saying he liked my profile. But what struck me was his photo. He had the most beautiful, haunting eyes, which seemed to look straight into my soul. I sat for ages looking into these eyes and knew I had to message him back. I can't remember what I said, but a few minutes later I got an email with his mobile number and a message saying I could phone him, but he would understand if I didn't want to. Two hours later I finally plucked up the courage to call. As the phone started ringing, I could feel my heart start to race. What if he didn't answer? Just as I was about to hang up, I heard a voice say, "Hello."

Steve spoke with a slight rural twang that reminded me of the TV series *The Darling Buds of May*, which was filmed locally.

"Hello," I gabbled. "It's Carol from Dateline."

Fortunately, Steve seemed pleased to hear from me and was fabulously easy to talk to. He told me he lived in a village in East Kent, in the heart of the county and worked on a farm. It sounded wonderful and we must have spoken for an hour. I was aware... the one thing I didn't mention in our conversation was Christopher's death.

We began to speak regularly and I vividly remember the phone call where he asked about Christopher.

"Carol," he said, "on your Dateline profile it says you have two children, but you only ever talk about Elizabeth."

I paused, worried how he would react, and then ploughed on, "My son Christopher died eight months ago," I said.

"I knew it was something like that," he said.

We spent the rest of the call talking about Christopher. He seemed very understanding. We continued to phone and text each other for quite a few weeks before we eventually decided to meet up. We arranged to meet for a drink in Rochester on a Saturday evening and that afternoon I went shopping with Elizabeth to buy something new to wear. I decided to play it safe and bought combat trousers (then in fashion) and a top. I certainly didn't want to do sexy on our first date! But I did treat myself to a new bottle of perfume.

As I was getting ready, I felt really nervous. What if, after all our lovely conversations, he was disappointed when he met me in the flesh? "What if I turn out to be a moose?" I had jokingly asked him. He laughed and said, "Well, I look like Shrek!"

Happily our first date went really well. We clicked straight away, immediately felt comfortable with one another and talked all evening. Things are looking up, I thought. But the following day my hopes for a new relationship were dashed when Steve phoned to say he didn't want to see me again. I was devastated and confused, we had got on so well, hadn't we? When I asked him why, he told me he didn't want to get hurt again. I struggled to understand and make him reconsider, but he wouldn't budge. He needed time to think. The sense of rejection was awful. Everybody told me to forget about him, but that was easier said than done.

Three weeks later I was lying awake in the early hours, I was still having difficulty sleeping. I got up to go to the loo and when I got back into bed I noticed my phone was showing a new text. It was from Steve. He apologised for texting me at 3 AM, evidently he wasn't sleeping either and he asked if I would give him another chance? He would completely understand if I didn't want anything more to do with him. I was delighted to hear from him and replied that I would call him the next day.

When we spoke, he told me he really liked me, but had not wanted to risk old relationship patterns repeating themselves. Now he realised he wanted to take that chance. We arranged to meet up and then spent the following weekend in a caravan in Dymchurch, Kent. When Steve told me about his past, I began to understand why he had been so scared to get into another relationship. It felt like I had finally met my soulmate.

At first we only dated on weekends until we developed a deeper relationship. I invited him to visit me at home so that he could meet Elizabeth. I knew that she would be cautious and I respected that, especially after the hurt that Mitch had caused at the end of our relationship.

I met Steve's oldest son and his partner Kate a few days before she gave birth to their first child. Steve phoned me at 3 AM, "I wanted you to be the first to know that I have become a grandad again. Kate has just had a little girl."

I felt so privileged to be the first one he told. The next time I met them both was in the postnatal ward of the William Harvey Hospital with their beautiful baby girl who was yet to be named. They eventually named her Roxanne.

I then met Steve's daughter Vanessa with her two children, Lauren and Jake, in July 2007. I was told that the reason Steve joined Dateline was that Lauren, who was only five years old, wanted to find her grandad a girlfriend. How lovely!

A few weeks after Roxanne was born, Steve and I went to a local animal park for the day. I had been introduced to Steve's mum and dad by then so we went to have Sunday tea with them and some of his family. As we both had to go to work the following day, I agreed to drive to Faversham on Monday evening to meet Steve for a drink. As I was driving on the M2, I began feeling unwell. Just before the turn off at Junction 6 I started to vomit. As I pulled off the junction there was a small rest stop. I pulled in and phoned Steve. I had the embarrassment of telling him that I had been sick in the car and could he bring a towel so I could clean myself up. There was no way I could drive to his house as Paul and Kate were there with their new baby and I didn't want to pass anything on to her. Ten minutes later he arrived with two towels. I was still throwing up out of the car door and saw Steve start to reach. I managed to clean myself up and covered myself in the clean towels.

"Sorry Steve, I need to go home," I said.

"You can't drive like that!" I could see he was concerned.

"I can't come home with you because of the baby. I will be ok."

Not convinced, I turned the car around and drove home while continuing to vomit. It was now coming out of both ends. I felt so ill. I did manage to text Steve to tell him that I had made it home. Eventually I managed to get to bed about 3 AM having showered three times and made a pathetic attempt to clean the bathroom. I'll leave the rest to your imagination...

The following morning I woke up to a text from Steve. "Oh my God, I've been so ill overnight."

It appears that we had got food poisoning from the lunch that we had at the animal park. A peacock had been running in and out of the café while the staff had been preparing and serving food. Elizabeth was clearly worried about me and became the perfect nurse. She went to the local pharmacy who advised that I should drink Sprite to help with rehydration. She also cleaned the bathroom and my car. I spent the next three days in bed. Steve was obviously built from stronger stuff and was eating toast the following day. Elizabeth was quite impressed that Steve had seen me in such a state so early in our relationship and didn't get put off!

In June 2007 Steve introduced me to banger racing and my first event was at Milden Hall Stadium in Suffolk. I then met his youngest son Lee who was racing. Steve used to race but now leaves it to the younger generation. It's certainly a very different world and to be honest I'm what is called a "fair weather fan." Although I enjoy the racing, I only like to go when it's warm and sunny. I can't bear standing for hours in the cold and rain.

I told Steve that I had always wanted to go to Longleat and he suggested that we spend a few days away in Wiltshire and incorporate a visit to Longleat. I phoned the tourist information to find out about places to stay and was told about a little place called "The Hobbit" in Norton Baven. It sounded amazing so I booked us to go away for a few days in October 2007. It was our first holiday together. The Hobbit was a self-contained extension to a family home and was just perfect. The second day we decided to visit Longleat. I have always loved animals and nature. I'm passionate about animal conservation and find being around animals so therapeutic.

> *"Until one has loved an animal, a part of one's soul remains unawakened."*
>
> - French poet Anatole France

We arrived at the park just before it opened and were first in the queue for the drive-through safari. It was a beautiful autumn day and I was feeling so excited. As we drove through, I just forgot about everything and immersed myself in the experience. I felt like I was in Africa. It was such a privilege to be so close to the animals, especially the majestic lions, which were just a couple of feet next to us.

Later, we enjoyed a boat trip and got to see Nico the gorilla who lived on Gorilla Island (apparently, he also had his own TV!). Whilst on the boat we also got to feed the sea lions. We ended our brilliant day getting lost in the maze. I was beginning to think that we would never find our way out especially as I have absolutely no sense of direction at the best of times. Thankfully Steve managed to get us out! Apparently, it's the largest maze in Britain. It was after this that we decided to get a little black and white cat, who we call Poppy.

During our early months as a couple, Christopher was never very far from my thoughts. I had learnt from Mary that the practice of praying for loved ones does not stop when those loved ones pass on; therefore, Catholics frequently light candles for the dead. I would often seek solace in a local Catholic Church where I would sit to pray and light a candle for my son. Steve would come into the church with me and just sit quietly until I was ready to leave. In the early days this gave me great comfort.

The first time Steve visited Christopher's gravestone with me was in January 2008. We decided to light a Chinese lantern in his memory. Unfortunately, the wind wasn't very helpful and sent the lantern towards a tree at the edge of the cemetery that overlooked some houses. Suddenly the lantern hooked onto a branch and set light to it. I was terrified the burning branch would be swept up by the wind and land close to the houses, setting them on fire. I shouted at Steve to climb the tree and put the lantern out. In my panic I reached up with a stick to try and unhook the lantern. Suddenly I heard Steve cry out. When I turned to see whatever was wrong he was standing covered in hot ashes. Understandably he did not look happy.

"What the bloody hell did you do that for?"

"I'm so sorry I didn't want the houses to catch fire."

"It doesn't matter about me."

Thankfully he wasn't hurt.

"I'm sorry babe, I wanted to do something special for you and Christopher." He was genuinely upset.

"Steve, it's ok. Christopher is up there having a great laugh at our expense. He had such a saucy sense of humour. Believe me, he is loving this."

As we drove out of the cemetery, I could hear Christopher's infectious laugh.

Living in the country, the skies are amazingly clear. One night I was very upset and Steve looked up to the sky and saw the brightest star ever. He comforted me, saying that whilst

Christopher was gone, he was that star, always watching and caring.

In April 2008 after we had been together a year, Steve asked me to get engaged. We were sitting in the kitchen finishing breakfast and he just dropped it into the conversation. I knew that I loved him and didn't hesitate in saying yes. Elizabeth's friend who was a jeweller found the perfect ring for me – a white gold solitaire. We officially got engaged over the May bank holiday weekend.

When Steve and I decided to move in together, my dad was a bit apprehensive. I know he found my move to Faversham quite hard, as it was a half an hour drive away, you would have thought that I'd gone to Australia. He had become dependent on me after Christopher passed away as he was now quite frail and unable to go out by himself. I continued to see Dad regularly, taking him out for a drink a couple of times a week. He really looked forward to our evenings out and was able to catch up with old friends at his local pub.

In the spring of 2009, Steve and I went on a family trip to Scotland for two weeks with his brother Robert, sister-in-law Jackie, and two of their daughters Sophie and Rebecca. Steve's mum and dad also came. We stayed at a Parkdean holiday camp near Pitlochry. During our visit we drove through the snow-capped mountains in the Trossachs National Park. The scenery was breathtaking and unlike anything I had seen before. I felt a strong spiritual connection with the mountains and surrounding landscape.

We stopped at the edge of Loch Tummel and had a barbecue by the water's edge. I just felt immersed in the surroundings. I listened to the water gently lapping against the shore and breathed in the clean air. It was definitely mother nature at her best and for a few hours I was able to feel some inner peace. While we were away, Steve and I celebrated the second anniversary of our meeting. Steve decided to take me out on the water and hired a rowing boat! He rowed out to the middle of the lake to me singing "Oh Life on the Ocean Waves." I hadn't laughed so much in ages.

One time, while we were out touring, we came across an old church. It was the ruins of Balquhidder Old Church in Sterling and turned out to be where Rob Roy was buried. We stopped and had a look round. I understood the church was not in regular use and only opened for special services. I suddenly noticed a strong smell of incense which I remember from when I attended Catholic mass. When I mentioned it to Steve, he said he couldn't smell anything. I'm not sure what the spiritual meaning of incense is, except that it's associated with prayer, but I strongly believe that it was a sign from Christopher that he was close to me.

On 8 April 2010 I got a phone call at work from my dad's neighbour saying she was worried about him. She hadn't heard him moving about that morning and after getting no answer when she knocked on his door, she had let herself in with the spare key that he had given her. She found him lying on the sofa still in his pyjamas and he appeared very unwell. He was coughing badly and bringing up mucus. I called the paramedics before leaving work to be with him. I also phoned Con who lived closer and he said he would go to check on my dad and wait until I got there. When I arrived, Dad was arguing with the paramedics who wanted him to go to hospital. He could be so stubborn at times.

It wasn't until the following day that he finally agreed to go after some coercion from me.

Once in hospital he was diagnosed with pneumonia and deteriorated quite quickly. Towards the end he struggled to speak, but before he passed away, his last words to me were, "I love you."

Those words were so precious.

I was devastated to lose Dad. With mum's passing in 1993, I now had to sell the family home and it felt like the final link to my parents and Christopher had gone. So, when the money came through from the sale of the house, Steve and I used some of the money to invest in a motorhome. We've had some wonderful times over the years in our "Norman Bus." Steve named it in memory of my dad.

The first time we went away, we spent the weekend in the New Forest. Being novice motorhome campers, we were totally unprepared! The first site we pitched up at was a small area of woodland known as Ashurst Wood and didn't require hook up. It was beautiful with forest ponies roaming freely on site. The second day we moved onto a site called Setthorns. This was completely different. Trees and bushes separated the pitches which created a completely private and tranquil feel in the heart of the forest. This site had an electric hook up which proved to be quite daunting. However, a lovely lady called Barbara who lived on the site showed us how to set it up. Once we knew what to do, it was so easy and we eventually laughed about how complex it had appeared to be. It meant we had luxuries like hot water, an electric kettle, and a TV.

We had such a lovely weekend and felt so de-stressed. Steve said he had the best night's sleep ever, as it was so peaceful.

If I wasn't prepared for the rollercoaster of emotions I experienced following Christopher's death, I was even more unnerved by the backlash I experienced nearly six years later. I suppose in order not to be overwhelmed by pain at the time, I managed to put some of my feelings on hold, which ultimately meant it took me longer to work through the cycle of grief. People do mourn in different ways and although there are recognised stages of grief, not everyone will go through them in the same order.

By the start of 2012 I was feeling very tired and run down. I put this down to being stressed about arranging our wedding in April. I was also very unhappy in my job and looking for a change, but what I was experiencing was more than common or garden stress. Essentially, I was hit from behind by a tidal wave of repressed emotions, which brought me to the verge of a nervous breakdown.

I began to have the most horrendous nightmares in which I was trying desperately to find Christopher and calling out his name. They were followed by flashbacks to Christopher's death, where I would see him lying lifeless on the hospital bed. My rising stress levels meant I would also burst into tears over the simplest things. At work I was struggling to cope and dreaded getting up in the morning, when inevitably I would wake with a knot of tension and a cold, sick feeling in my stomach. The final straw came one morning when my manager asked me to do something for her. Instead of just doing it, I found myself starting to panic and burst into tears. The sick feeling in my stomach took over. She took me into her office and I can remember her being very kind. She had known something was wrong for a while.

"Carol, why don't you go home?" she said, and made me promise I would see my GP. Then I phoned Steve and told him what was happening.

"Ok babe, drive carefully," was all he said – he didn't seem at all surprised. On top of everything else, I now felt a complete failure and couldn't make any sense of what I was feeling or what was happening to me. I was soon to be married to a wonderful man and Elizabeth was doing well in her business – I was so proud of her. Although Christopher had passed on six years before, it felt like it had only just happened.

Instead of going straight home, I parked my car at the top of a hill near Dover Castle. As I trudged up the hill, I felt like I had lead weights on my feet. Then I drove to the local garden centre. I remember sitting in the car in the middle of the car park while it poured with rain. The black sky mirrored my feelings exactly. I felt inexplicably scared and very lonely. That evening I went to see my doctor. She explained that what I was experiencing was a delayed grief reaction. She explained that the distressing dreams and flashbacks were symptoms of post-traumatic stress disorder (PTSD) as a result of losing a child. She believed my upcoming wedding could have triggered it. It was not only about losing Christopher but also associated with the loss of both my parents. She signed me off work for two months. I was not a nice person to be around in the following weeks. Constantly bad-tempered, I often vented my anger at Steve. Sometimes I would swear and rant at a photograph of Christopher.

Dad had been such a significant figure in Christopher's life, especially after my mother died. Now I couldn't seem to separate him and Christopher in my head. I decided to contact Cruse Bereavement for counselling and had weekly meetings with a wonderful lady called Olwen who helped me work through all the feelings I had previously suppressed. Although I had counselling immediately following Christopher's death, I now realise that I had not allowed myself to open up and properly work through my feelings.

The brilliant thing about Steve is that he never lets me give up, no matter how bad things get. If timing is everything, then I met him at one of the worst times in my life, a lesser man would have walked away. I know Steve has had his own struggles and hurt in life, and while such events can make many people bitter and resentful, adversity has only helped him to develop empathy and understanding. Don't get me wrong, he's not all sweetness and light. When people cross him he can be very unforgiving. If you take the time to look beyond his tough exterior you'll see the caring and loving man that got me through some of my darkest times. Steve sometimes had to take a "tough love" approach with me. I remember on one occasion I was feeling particularly low. He had tried everything to lift my mood and was starting to get very frustrated.

Suddenly I heard him say, "I thought it was Christopher who died, not you." That got my attention.

"What did you just say?" I asked, annoyed.

"You're acting as if it was you who died," he clarified. I could see the pain in his eyes. But he was right, and at the time it was what I needed to hear.

Mothering Sunday is always tough. The first time after Steve and I got together, Elizabeth sent me a beautiful bouquet of flowers. Unfortunately she was working on Sunday, which meant I wouldn't see her so I was feeling a bit upset as I went upstairs for a bath. But when I came downstairs after my bath, Elizabeth's flowers had been joined by a basket of plants and a card. I looked at Steve.

"They're from Christopher," he said. "He wants you to know that he's still thinking of you."

The plants in the basket were gorgeous and Steve had signed the card from Christopher. I could feel the tears welling up, it was such a lovely thing to do. Now every Mothering Sunday, thanks to Steve, I still receive a gift from both of my children. Christopher would definitely approve.

It's typical of Steve to think of me in that way. Our relationship does have its ups and downs. I am mostly quite laid back, while Steve likes things to be more organised, so we do argue at times and as we both have fiery tempers, though our arguments sound worse than they are. But we also have so much in common, including our love of nature.

The places we tour in the "Norman Bus" reflect this. We have been to the New Forest, Cornwall, Devon, The Lake and Peak Districts, as well as local sites in the South East. It might sound like a cliché, but Steve has been my rock. My journey has not been an easy one, but he has been there with me every step of the way.

In November 2012, I decided to take a break from working and set up my own life coaching business. It was also at this time that we got our own little brindle Staffie puppy who we called Buster Bear (named after Arthur Bear). He was such a bundle of energy and brought so much life to our home. Poppy, our cat, immediately put him in his place, so he knew his pecking order.

Buster is now eight and Poppy is 11 years old. They both get on so well, cuddling up together on the sofa in the evening. Over the last few years, any time I am feeling low they are able to boost my mood and ease my depression and grief. I have heard cats being described as nature's tranquilliser. Poppy is a very independent cat but sits on the arm of the chair demanding to be stroked. I love listening to her purring and it seems to ease my stress. Staffordshire Bull Terriers (Staffies) are such loving dogs despite their bad reputation. Buster loves his cuddles and I find having hugs and stroking him helps to calm me when I feel stressed or anxious. He does get a little jealous of Poppy and will nudge her out of the way if he thinks she is getting more attention than him! Together they make such good companions.

Elizabeth was always a happy, easy child; here she is on our trip to Battle Abbey

CHAPTER 7
~
ELIZABETH

Written 5 August 1988, 6:15pm

<u>Elizabeth</u>
Today I've gained a little optimism.
It's been a lazy few hours.
The evening sun is really quite pleasant.
The kids are behaving.
The house is cleaner.
I'm indulging in sentimental music.
And I don't even feel like crying.
"Do I talk too much Mummy?" Elizabeth is asking.
"No darling." And I give her a cuddle anyway.
She tells me about the fairies.
"Maybe they're flying into space."
And I remember back as a child,
When my imagination was as wonderful
and innocent as hers.
Keep it my darling. For as long as you can.
Now Con is home and the mood is broken.
There's dinner to prepare.
Shopping to be done.
And shouldn't I go to the loo.

The night her brother died, Elizabeth was just 26 years old. As we stood by his bedside in the hospital room, I could see how hard she was struggling to hold back her tears. I didn't really know how to comfort her, she was a very private person and struggled to show her emotions. I knew if I put my arm around her, she would probably freeze.

"I wasn't a very good sister was I?" she said.

During the last year Christopher had become something of a recluse, so I couldn't allow her to go on believing that. When we visited him, he would either shut himself away in his room or he had been asleep.

"Christopher didn't allow you to be a good sister, he'd stopped letting anyone get close to him recently."

We remained in silence for a few minutes before joining the others in the hospital lounge.

Growing up as an only child was very lonely for me and I always longed for a brother or sister. Unfortunately, my brother was stillborn as my mum had undiagnosed pre-eclampsia. She was so ill afterwards she was advised not to have any more children. So I was determined that I would have more than one child.

Elizabeth Mary Ring was born at 6 PM on 17 September 1980, after a fairly straightforward labour.

The whole experience of pregnancy and childbirth with Elizabeth could not have been more different for me than it was with Chris. This time Con was present for the birth of his daughter and was the first one to hold her. As the midwife put her into his arms, I remember she deposited meconium all over him. I laughed, "That's what she thinks of you." I was so excited to be a mother for the second time. The midwife put her in a hospital cot while she went off to do something. Elizabeth just lay there kicking her legs and staring at us. I watched her in amazement. This was what people meant when they described the joy, exhilaration, and elation of childbirth!

The next day in the postnatal ward I heard a familiar voice. "Where's mummy, where's mummy?" It was Christopher coming to say hello to his sister for the first time. Chris was three and a half when Elizabeth was born and, bless his heart, he thought she would be an instant playmate for him. When I introduced him to her, he looked into the cradle in disappointment. What use could she be to him?

Although I still suffered from postpartum depression after Elizabeth was born, it was nowhere near as severe as it was with Chris. I bonded with her immediately and coped much better in the immediate aftermath. As a toddler Elizabeth was very strong willed. The couple next door had two little boys of similar ages to my two. Elizabeth was very much the tomboy and would always join in with their games.

Sibling Rivalry

There was a lot of sibling rivalry between Christopher and Elizabeth as they were growing up. Christopher had three years of sole focus of attention up until Elizabeth was born. Regression and jealousy in children is very common with a new baby in the house. I think he felt pushed out. He started to wet the bed again. I tried to make special time for him and reassure him that he was still loved. I felt guilty that I had bonded so quickly with my daughter and wished it had been like that when Christopher was born.

Growing up they were very different in temperament. Elizabeth seemed more confident and outgoing than Christopher. He was more like me as a child. He was quite shy when around a group of other children. He sometimes seemed unsure about what he was supposed to do. This often led to conflict between them. They were always bickering and I found it hard to know when to get involved.

As an only child, I had never experienced sibling rivalry. Sometimes their arguments became physical and because Christopher was bigger he was always the winner.

I remember one occasion, when they were both sitting on the sofa watching TV, Elizabeth, who was about four years old, suddenly hit her brother over the head with a cup. Con and I sat there in amazement as Christopher burst into tears. As I tried to comfort him an unrepentant Elizabeth sat smirking. Of course I told her off for doing it, but I guess she was getting her own back at her big brother.

Leading up to Christmas 1986, Christopher came home from school with some Christmas decorations that he had made. He was so proud.

"Mum, can we make our Christmas decorations this year instead of buying them?" It sounded like a brilliant idea. Elizabeth wanted to make some, too.

After a trip to Woolworths we made lots of paper chains and things for the Christmas tree. Christopher and Elizabeth were so excited to see their efforts. Con hung the paper chains on the ceiling while we decorated the Christmas tree. The entire house was decorated with homemade decorations. It really made Christmas that year.

In January 1987 it snowed for four days. Our car was buried under a white blanket and the snow came halfway up the back door. Con was working in London and as the trains weren't running he couldn't get home. The schools were all closed so the children were at home. They loved it and built a snowman in the garden. My dad trudged through all the heavy snow to give me some bread and milk as I was snowed in. Christopher and Elizabeth squealed with laughter as they bombarded their grandad with snowballs. These memories are so precious.

When the children were growing up, we had a menagerie of animals. At one time we had five cats, two rabbits, two guinea pigs, and a gerbil. Everyone warned me that all their care would be left to me but it was Elizabeth who, from a very young age, took charge of feeding and cleaning out of the hutches. She never had to be asked.

When she was eight years old somebody at school told her on Halloween that the witches would come and take her rabbit Snowy. Snowy's hutch was kept in the garage and she pleaded with me to let her have him in the bedroom overnight. However, Con and I told her that Snowy would be perfectly safe in the garage. She went to bed a little concerned, but I got the impression that her beloved Snowy was going to be just fine. During the night, I heard a scraping noise coming from her bedroom. When I went to have a look, Snowy was running around the bedroom floor and Elizabeth was fast asleep. Elizabeth had sneaked out to the garage after we had all gone to bed! I didn't have the heart to put Snowy back in his hutch so I covered the floor with newspaper to catch any droppings. Needless to say, in the morning Snowy was perfectly safe and hadn't been taken by the witches.

At nine years old, Elizabeth became very aware of battery farming and animal cruelty. She made the decision to become a vegetarian. It was something that I had been thinking about for a couple of years and decided to make the transition with her. We were met with a lot of criticism and one woman told me that she thought it was disgusting that I had allowed my nine year old daughter to stop eating meat. She said that it would lead to all sorts of health problems. However, as a responsible mother, I looked into it carefully to make sure Elizabeth would still get all the proper nutrients. Vegetarianism has since become a way of life for both of us.

Con and Christopher were a little bemused that we had both become vegetarians and probably thought it was going to be a five minute wonder. Con was always a good cook and did make the effort to make some very tasty vegetarian meals when he was home, which Christopher was happy to dig into despite his protests that it didn't have any meat in it. I remember making a vegetarian stew for dinner and he was adamant that he was not going to eat "rabbit food." When I started dishing it up he reluctantly agreed to try some. After having three bowlfuls he conceded with a cheeky grin that it was, "ok, I suppose."

In her teenage years Elizabeth became a bit of a rebel. When she was 14 she organised the abduction of the fairy on top of the Christmas tree in the main entrance of her school. She then sent a ransom note to her teachers. It was received in good spirits and she became somewhat notorious for it. When I worked for the education department in 2004, I visited the school and the staff there still remembered the incident with affection.

Looking back to the first couple of years after Christopher died it didn't feel like Elizabeth and I were very close. As I retreated into my own grief, Elizabeth must have felt the loss of her brother very deeply. Whilst they didn't always get on, Elizabeth loved her brother enormously. She believed that she would have a lifetime with her brother and we were both grieving in different ways. I have always worn my emotions on my sleeve whereas Elizabeth tends to keep her feelings to herself, I would sometimes forget that she was struggling with her own grief as well. I wasn't being selfish, I just found it difficult to be the healthy, emotional support to her that I had been before.

Everyone in the immediate family is affected when a family member has schizophrenia. It was not until recently that

I considered the impact Christopher's schizophrenia had on Elizabeth's early years. At times she must have felt Christopher had more of my attention than she did and her needs were not always being met. At times she struggled to understand what was happening to her brother and was confused by his behaviour. It must have been difficult to try to explain his illness to her friends when she didn't fully understand it herself.

"If only I had known as much about mental health when Chris was alive as I do now," she told me a few months ago.

Why would she have known? This was all new to her, I should have discussed it more with her and helped her to understand. Hindsight is a wonderful thing, but even though I was a mental health nurse, I had my own journey to go through. For this reason, I think it's important that the siblings of people enduring mental health difficulties also have support from outside groups.

It was Elizabeth's dream to work with animals when she got older. What she really wanted was a dog but her dad always said no. One Christmas I asked her what she wanted and she stated quite firmly, "a dog." When I told her she couldn't have a dog, she simply said, "I don't want anything then." Of course, she had Christmas presents that year, but she was so disappointed that she didn't get a dog.

My marriage to Con was coming to an enduring end and we were always arguing. As Christopher was staying with my dad it was Elizabeth who had to cope with us fighting, her brother wasn't there for support. She once told me it was like living in a battleground. When Con and I separated I went to live with my dad and Christopher whilst Elizabeth stayed with Con in the family home. I enquired about renting a house as I desperately wanted her to move in with me.

In the beginning Elizabeth believed that I would go back to her dad. She even went and got a new kitten thinking it might entice me back home. She didn't realise that this time the split was permanent. All the houses that I looked into renting stated "no animals." Elizabeth's animals were so important to her. Eventually she decided to continue living with Con. I know that Elizabeth wanted to come and live with me, but she wasn't prepared to leave her animals behind. I also felt that she had rejected me in some way. I had always assumed that no matter what happened she would choose to stay with me. It was me who wanted an end to my marriage and therefore I was responsible for leaving behind the daughter who I loved dearly. I felt so guilty and missed her so much.

As Christopher was already living with my dad when I moved in, I spent a lot of time with him. We would often stay up late after my dad had gone to bed and have long chats trying to put the world to rights.

I didn't realise Elizabeth was struggling until one evening I got a phone call from Con to say that he had received a letter saying she had been excluded from school for a week due to bad behaviour. He then found a note from her saying that she was so sorry she had let us down. She had left home and wasn't coming back.

Con and I had been separated for a year and I had just moved in with my new partner, Mitch. I wasn't aware of the letter from school until that moment, as correspondence only went back to the family home. It was so out of character for her as she had always been the model child. She was only 14 years old and I was frantic.

I called the police and they came to take a statement. Con and I were bewildered. We had no idea of what had been going on at school. My imagination was going wild about where she had gone and who she was with. Was she in any danger? To my annoyance, the police didn't appear too concerned.

"This often happens but most children usually come back home."

I didn't get any sleep that night and as soon as the school opened I was there demanding to know why I hadn't been informed that Elizabeth was having problems. I had been to the school when Con and I had separated to let them know what was going on and had asked to be kept informed of Elizabeth's progress. I went to the reception desk and insisted on knowing why they hadn't informed me of Elizabeth's exclusion.

"My daughter has been missing all night and the police have been looking for her. Why wasn't I informed that she had been excluded? I want to know why and I want to know now."

The lady at the reception became very flustered. "I'm so sorry, I can find out what happened."

She made a couple of phone calls and suddenly two members of staff appeared from different directions.

"Mrs. Ring, I'm so sorry, please come into the office." I slumped into the chair and burst into tears.

"Elizabeth has run away from home. She left a note saying she was so ashamed at being excluded and couldn't face me or her dad. Why wasn't I told?"

It turned out that the teacher I told about the changes in our domestic circumstances had not passed on the information and the school was not aware that Con and I had separated. They didn't have my new details. It turns out that this particular teacher was Elizabeth's head of year and was really empathetic.

"I'm really sorry you weren't informed. We had no idea of what was happening at home."

"But I met with her form tutor and she assured me that I would be kept informed of Elizabeth's progress."

"That teacher has left the school. She didn't pass on the information."

He explained that Elizabeth's behaviour in school had become a cause for concern and had eventually led to her fixed term exclusion. I had been so wrapped up in my marriage break up and Christopher's problems I hadn't noticed that my daughter might have been missing her mum. I felt so guilty. After I left the school I drove to my dad's in tears. About ten minutes after I arrived, my mobile phone rang and it was Elizabeth.

"Mum, I'm home. I'm so sorry I've really let you down. I'm so ashamed." By this time I was sobbing with relief.

"Elizabeth, just stay there. I'm coming round. I've been so scared for you."

"Mum, I'm ok," Elizabeth said.

"I'm on my way."

"Dad, I'm sorry, I've got to go, Elizabeth is home."

"Carol, calm down. Please drive safely."

I was shaking.

When I arrived I gave Elizabeth the biggest hug. "I've been so worried."

It turned out that she had been camping on the farm behind the house and hadn't been very far away at all. She had been scared about how I was going to react when I found out that she had been suspended from school. I reassured her that I loved her and that we could work through this. After this incident, I kept in close contact with the school and things slowly improved.

I feel like I lost valuable time with my daughter during her early teens. I believe that children need to spend one-to-one time with each parent after they split up. It wasn't always easy in the early days following our relationship breakup with emotions running very high, but I realised that I wasn't spending enough time with her. I wasn't being a good mother to either of my children and was focusing too much on my own needs.

I was 36 years old and with a new partner. Although I knew my marriage to Con was over, I still missed family life. I was like a fish out of water. I now had a wake up call, as their mum, and saw that my children needed me.

A few months later I had a phone call from Sue to say that her sister-in-law's dog had given birth to two puppies. It appears that she had gotten out of the garden when she was in season and they didn't even know she was pregnant until she went into labour. She wondered if I was interested in having one of the puppies for Elizabeth. She had a birthday coming up so I agreed to have one. When I told Elizabeth she was so excited.

That evening Sue took us to see the puppies. They were Bearded Collie cross and the most enormous puppies I have ever seen. Elizabeth made her choice and named her Lucy. Eight weeks later Elizabeth was able to take her puppy home. I wondered how Con was going to react, but he fell in love with her instantly.

Elizabeth told me recently that after I left she gave up on her education and found it hard to focus on her school work. It didn't seem important to her any more. I feel really sad about that, but I am glad that it hasn't held her back in achieving her ambition to work with animals. I was so pleased when she started doing some voluntary work at a local veterinarian. It gave her a focus again.

She obviously faced her own emotional battle after Christopher died in her own private way. She lost a brother and with no other siblings to share her thoughts with, she must have felt so alone. At times during the early days I know that I wasn't always there for her, but I try as hard as I can now to be there for her emotionally.

As a mother I couldn't be more proud of my daughter Elizabeth. She left Battersea Dogs Home and started her own successful dog business. She works so hard and is very diligent in what she does. When Arthur died, Elizabeth and I were heartbroken. Elizabeth was adamant that she wasn't going to get another dog but a few months later she adopted another dog from Battersea – a beautiful little Staffie-cross called Sparkle.

Christopher and Elizabeth having fun on the beach during a holiday in Somerset

Chapter 8

~

A New Normal

Life is certainly different without Christopher, but I have started to enjoy it again. Coming to terms with my son's illness and death hasn't been easy and has pushed me beyond the limits of what I thought I could bear, but I've finally reached a point where I feel I can share my journey.

By writing about what our family went through with Christopher, perhaps I can help other bereaved parents come to terms with this most unnatural of situations.

Someone asked me recently if I had coined the phrase "new normal." Sadly I can't take credit for it. The phrase became popular around the time of the 2008 financial crash to describe the new, straitened circumstances to which many were having to adjust. My "new normal" was the point where my life felt worthwhile again. The downward trajectory had stopped and although Christopher's absence remained a gaping hole, finally I could believe he was at peace.

How did this resolution come about? Several events in the years following Christopher's death helped, although sometimes I didn't appreciate their significance until long afterwards.

One evening, when I'd been going out with Steve for about a year, we went for a drink in our local pub where they were hosting a psychic evening. On impulse I decided to go along. As I took my seat she asked me if I'd lost a child. Confused, I stuttered, "Eh? No, I haven't." I wasn't giving anything away.

"That's strange," she said, "Because I have someone here with me. I must have it wrong." She started talking about other things and then said, "I'm feeling very confused. There's definitely a young man with me who says you're his mum."

I came clean. "I'm sorry," I said, "I wasn't being entirely truthful. I did lose my son recently."

The medium looked relieved.

"So, you were testing me," she said, "I don't blame you. Your son is here with me now. He's telling me he's happy and you're not to feel guilty. His death was all his own fault."

She went on to tell me something about Christopher which no one else could possibly have known. She also used the same language he would have used to describe Steve and said he approved of him. I realise many people are sceptical about this kind of thing, but I honestly believe Chris sent me a message that night and I still gain a lot of comfort from it. I see nothing wrong with exploring different aspects of spirituality, providing you temper it with a good dose of common sense. It's something that I've gained motivation from. I have since done a course in Tarot card reading. I mainly use the cards for personal and psychic development.

Soon after the psychic reading, I started a new National Health Service (NHS) job working with substance misuse clients. To me this was just coincidence, but Steve is more inclined to see it as something I was destined to do given Christopher's history. I certainly enjoyed the challenge and learnt a lot about the nature of addiction. Many of the clients I worked with also had mental health problems and they used drugs to cope with their feelings.

During my work with this client group, I came across the concept of life coaching in a nursing journal and decided to find out more about it. It seemed a great way to support people to take control of their own lives, something many of us find difficult to do. After looking into it a little more, I felt life coaching was something I could usefully do. As well as helping me in my work with addicts, the training would enable me to start a private coaching practice. Steve was initially a bit apprehensive, but eventually agreed to support me. Today, my life coaching work inspires me in so many ways. I really feel I am making a difference to my clients, empowering them to negotiate obstacles that may be holding them back and to live their lives in more positive and fulfilling ways.

As a life coach, I mostly work with people who have issues such as stress, anxiety, and depression, which affect their emotional wellbeing. My role is to help them find their own solutions towards positive mental health and thus allow them to move forward with their life. I firmly believe taking care of your mental health is just as important as eating, sleeping, and exercise, but it is something that so many of us neglect until something unexpected happens that forces us to take stock.

Just before Christmas 2014, I was at a small business fair in Faversham when suddenly life coach Kerry Hales with microphone in hand boomed across the hall, "Carol Macey why are you not life coaching bereaved mothers?"

I had attended one of her amazing workshops in the summer and she knew all about my history. I had discussed the possibility of coaching bereaved mothers but hadn't done anything about it. So I asked myself the same question, "Why am I not life coaching bereaved mothers?" At that point I had been a life coach for four years working with a wide variety of clients. It's something that I continue to take forward. I have coached several clients who have experienced child bereavement and have realised that the journey is purely a personal one and different for everyone. There are no hard and fast rules, but comfort can be gained from sharing.

It hasn't been an easy journey.

It's important for me to stress that this is my personal journey. I want Christopher's relatively short life to have been for a reason and to have some purpose to it. I want to keep his memory alive.

I suppose I could use my skills to become more of a business coach and significantly increase my earning potential, but I wouldn't be being true to myself or to Christopher. I decided to commence hypnotherapy training in 2014 to add another therapeutic tool to my belt in order to help my clients with their anxiety and stress. I can remember someone of a similar age to me asking, "Why are you taking on something so big at your age? I just want to start winding down now."

Why would I want to wind down? I still feel I have so much more to give in memory of Chris. Unfortunately, I had to defer my training due to a major hip problem that resulted in a hip replacement. Prior to my operation I was in a great deal of pain and my mobility was very poor. I was starting to feel depressed and for a while something had to go. Fortunately I had a lot of support from Steve and Elizabeth. My friends and work colleagues were all wonderful, too. I got through it and the operation was a great success. While I was recuperating I spent a lot of time writing this book. I am looking forward to finishing my hypnotherapy training in the near future.

My values have changed. I no longer go shopping at Bluewater buying clothes I don't need or can't afford. I now live in the country and would prefer to go for a walk around the orchard with Steve and our dog, Buster. Having been quite immobile for a few years I cherish this even more now. To be honest, I am quite lazy at times and have to be encouraged to go on walks by Steve, but I am getting better.

One night I was feeling quite tired and Steve said: "I know it's a big ask but you still have your boots on and I want to show you something."

"No Steve, it's late and I'm tired."

"Please, it will be gone in the morning," he pleaded. I eventually gave in and we went for a moonlight walk with Buster. We walked a little way into the orchard near where we live and he shone his torch onto an object.

"Wow!" I said.

Someone had carved a huge fox from a tree trunk using a chainsaw. It was amazing.

"I knew you'd like it," Steve said.

If I hadn't gone on that walk I wouldn't have seen it. And Steve was right, it wasn't there the next day.

Why I do the work I'm doing now

In my role as a mental health nurse, I am sometimes faced with situations that bring back memories of Christopher. This can happen if a client presents as delusional and is experiencing loss of motivation and social withdrawal. If a client has similar characteristics to Christopher then I have to acknowledge that this could evoke memories or feelings that may be difficult to deal with. My strength is that I'm very self-aware and usually know if this is happening. People at work are aware of my history and I am very lucky that I work with a very caring team. I couldn't do the work I do without the support I receive from my colleagues and in return, I do my best to support them.

I feel my experience of being a carer to my son has really helped my role. I can empathise with the families whose loved ones have psychosis. I have shared this with families when I feel it's appropriate and it will help them. I once had a mother break down on me as she had lost her oldest daughter in a road accident and was now having to take care of her son. I disclosed to her that I had lost Chris and understood what she was going through. She really appreciated this.

Part of my role is to help people who are relapsing and are experiencing impaired judgement caused by psychosis. They might be in immediate danger of harming themselves or others and have no insight into what is happening to them. If a client is at risk and refuses to go into hospital voluntarily, I then have them assessed under the Mental Health Act for their own safety. This may result in my client being detained under said Act in order to ensure that they receive the right care and treatment to aid recovery. Whenever I have been involved in this process I am always clear in my own mind that it is in the best interest of the client, just like it was when Christopher was in Medway Hospital when he first became ill. I can continue to support them while they remain in hospital and have a role in their discharge planning. I then work with them when they are well enough to go home.

One of the main reasons I work in the area I do is because I like helping people to reach their full potential, especially those who are experiencing mental health problems. I promote the importance of self-care and help them to develop resilience to manage their lives in a positive way. I recognise that this can be really challenging for some clients. It is important for me to go that extra mile for a client to help them and their families to get the best outcome without becoming over involved.

Chapter 9
~
8 October 2016

8 October 2016 marked the 10th anniversary of Christopher's passing. As it was such a significant anniversary, I found the lead up to it especially painful.

Some people don't seem to understand it doesn't matter how much time has gone by since losing your precious child, your heart still aches. Although 10 years on, I am more prepared for the emotional wallop when something triggers off a memory and I know that it's completely normal.

Steve works on a farm and we always have a holiday in October when the harvest is finished. This year we went to Cornwall in the "Norman Bus" with our dog Buster. Usually we would have left on Saturday, but I did not want to be travelling on Christopher's anniversary, so instead we started our journey in the early hours of Friday 7 October. We arrived late afternoon at a campsite in Mullion to the amazing sight of a Volkswagen convention. The campers were so friendly and made such a fuss of Buster.

I wanted to remember Christopher in a special way and asked Steve if we could go to the unspoilt fishing harbour of Porthleven the following day. We had been there last year and I had fond memories of our visit.

When we arrived at the harbour the sun was shining and it was really warm for October. I felt sad, but I was feeling really close to Christopher. We sat outside a bar with Buster having a drink while overlooking the harbour, watching the fishing boats coming in with their catch. Buster kept barking at the seagulls that were pecking at the food dropped by passersby. I felt like Christopher had sent the sun to make the day easier for me.

I reflected on how much my life had changed in the last ten years. I think Christopher would have approved, but how I would have loved for him to have been part of it. I'm going to be honest and say that given his mental health issues and lack of insight, I find it really difficult to imagine how Christopher's life would be now if he had lived. I can't even think about the milestones he never achieved like graduating from university, getting married, or becoming a father.

As we walked around the harbour we came across a little beach that was packed with people and dogs. I left Steve videoing the harbour and I walked down a small ramp leading onto the beach comprised of a small sandy cove with lots of rocks. It was an amazing sight, people having picnics on the beach in October. I couldn't believe how warm and sunny it was. I needed to phone Elizabeth to tell her. When we spoke it's as if we didn't need to talk about what day it was. I just wanted to hear her voice. I told her about the beach and how beautiful the weather was. She said she was pleased and hoped that I enjoyed my holiday. A little later she sent me a text "Love U, I do remember it's Chris's anniversary xx."

I looked up from my phone to Steve and Buster walking down the ramp. It was Buster's first experience of a sandy beach as he is used to pebbles. His first reaction was to dig and have a poo. Just as well I remembered the poo bags. I found myself giggling as I picked up the offending article. How Christopher would have laughed at this.

A man came running over to me and asked if I had any more bags. "My dog has just pooed and I don't have any bags with me!"

"You are in luck. I've got a spare one," I laughed. He was so grateful!

Suddenly I felt like a child again.

"Steve, I'm going to have a paddle in the sea."

"Really?!" he cried.

I walked down the sea and sat on a rock to take my shoes and socks off. Steve pulled me up and I stood watching the waves as they hit the rocks. There was a gentle breeze and the sun was glistening on the sea. It felt so inviting. As I walked into the water I found myself sinking down and felt the wet sand between my toes. The water lapped against my feet, it was so cold but it felt fabulous!

I tried to tempt Buster in to join me but he wasn't having any of it. He is scared of water and decided the Labrador further up the beach was more interesting. I heard Steve call him back as he retracted his extendable lead. I came out of the sea to sit on the rock and allowed the warm sun to dry my feet. We decided to go back to the pub where we had a drink and lunch as we knew it was dog friendly. I had a chick pea curry and Steve had a prawn baguette with all the trimmings. They were amazing! After lunch we walked further along the harbour and I saw a crystal shop. I went in while Steve sat on the bench outside with Buster looking out to sea. Inside I was immediately attracted to an amethyst cross on a silver chain. Amethyst is my birthstone. Apparently it's a stone of psychic awareness, meditation, peace, and healing. I went outside to tell Steve. Bless him he got out his wallet and gave me some money.

"Go and buy it for Christopher."

I was close to tears.

"Go on. Hurry up."

I picked up the cross and took it to the till. The lady at the counter smiled as she put it into a lovely pink, silver, and turquoise gift bag.

"Beautiful isn't it."

"Yes, it is."

Later that day we drove to Mullion Cove and parked on the cliff top in front of the Mullion Hotel. The water was perfectly still and looked like a mirror. I stepped out of the motorhome and sat on a bench. The view was spectacular and it was so peaceful. I closed my eyes and thought about Christopher. My love for him will last forever, just as my grief will last forever because I can't have one without the other.

> *"Grief is the last act of love we can give to those we loved. Where there is deep grief, there is great love."*
>
> ~Anonymous

I had been dreading this day for weeks but this was the perfect place to remember him.

When we arrived back at the holiday park the Volkswagen convention was still there and the campsite had a wonderful atmosphere. One of the campers was trying out his new drone and it became the topic of conversation. Apparently it cost £2000! As I sat outside with a large glass of Pinot enjoying the evening sunshine, I decided to phone Con. He sounded a bit subdued when he answered but seemed to immediately cheer up at the sound of my voice.

"Hi, I thought I'd phone as it's Chris's 10th anniversary," I explained.

"I know."

He went silent for a few seconds. "Anyway, how are you doing?" Con asked.

"Ok I guess considering what day it is."

"Me too," he said.

"We are in Cornwall with the motorhome."

"Really? What's the weather like down there?"

"It's beautiful and sunny. I went paddling in the sea this morning."

I heard him chuckle.

"Do you remember when we took the kids away and your bikini top came off in the sea? The kids thought it was really funny."

"Yes, I do." I laughed, "I was a lot younger and slimmer then. Wouldn't be seen in one now!"

It was lovely to be reminded of my beautiful children when they were young. It's so easy to forget the good memories when you are grieving. As I finished my phone call Steve came out of the motor home.

"I don't want to go out tonight, the football is on the telly, England are playing Malta."

I smiled. How Christopher loved his football. "That's ok," I said.

The final score was England 2 Malta 0. Great result. The perfect end to a perfect celebration.

Chapter 10

~

Therapy

What is recovery?

In January 2015 I started working as a community mental health nurse after seven years in the substance misuse field. The work I do now is more focused on early intervention and was not around when Christopher was diagnosed with serious mental health problems. For me, my role has a more holistic approach and I work with clients between 14-65 years old with first episode psychosis. It has definitely been a steep learning curve for me and has been personally very challenging. Did I do the best for my son when he was ill? Yes, probably, based on what I knew then, but if I was supporting Christopher today, things would be very different.

Back then my expectations were for him to be well, therefore symptom free and leading a so-called normal life. Realistically that was never going to happen due to his lack of insight and an enduring mental health problem. What he needed was help to manage his symptoms and relapses, so that he would feel more in control of his life and it would become more meaningful for him. When I reflect on this, I have a choice in whether I let myself be overcome with guilt and believe that in some way I could have prevented my beloved son's premature death, or channel this knowledge into something more positive.

I spent a long time feeling guilty about my son both when he was alive and after he passed away, but I don't believe that Christopher would have wanted that guilt to destroy me. That would mean there had been no purpose to his life, when in fact he'd had such a profound impact on everyone who knew him.

I feel that my experience of being the parent of a child with mental health issues informs my work with clients and their families. When speaking with a colleague, we both agreed that the medical model has its benefits but is no longer seen as the whole answer.

The National Institute for Health and Care Excellence (NICE), which provides national guidance and advice to improve health and social care, now recommends Cognitive Behavioural Therapy (BFT) for psychosis.

In 2015 I did a five day course in BFT. This is a programme that can be used to work with families when a member has mental health problems. It helps to educate and reduce stress within the family environment (Jhadray et al., 2015). During one of the feedback sessions I felt it was appropriate at that point to disclose about my own experience as a parent and became quite tearful. Suddenly I couldn't finish my words. "I'm sorry, I've got to leave the room."

I was feeling so stupid and embarrassed. A colleague came out of the training to make sure that I was ok and I kept finding myself apologising even though he reassured me that I didn't need to. To my surprise, during the tea break many of the other trainees on the course thanked me for being so open and felt it had made a positive contribution to the training. One said, "You are so brave to talk about your experiences. This is real isn't it?"

I truly believe that this intervention would have been beneficial to my family years earlier. Life could be very stressful especially when Christopher was relapsing and it would have helped us not only support my son better, but would have also helped us all understand the impact our own behaviour was having on the situation.

There is another intervention called Open Dialogue. I can't profess to have any professional or personal experience of it. However, those of my colleagues who have or are doing the training appear very positive about it. Open Dialogue was first developed in Finland and is a new approach that is for people who are suffering from a mental health crisis such as psychosis or suicidal ideation.

It is in the early stages of development in the UK and the NHS is running four pilot studies which include the NHS trust that I work for. A small team in Kent has been established as part of the research project. I was very interested in finding out more about it and recently spoke to one of my colleagues who has completed the Open Dialogue training. This colleague informed me that there is evidence from the studies in Finland that it is very positive and has increased recovery rates. People who have had open dialogue are less dependent on medication and a higher rate of people are returning to employment. The current randomised trial in the UK is looking to see if it produces similar results.

He informed me that it is still in the early stages of development in the UK and not widely available. The criteria for people being referred to the team is that they have to be present in crisis, live in a certain geographical area (Canterbury or Medway), and have not been seen in services for at least six months. The team provides continuity of care and the aim is to see the person presenting in crisis within 24 hours. All meetings with the client generally take place within the home or a place of their choice. These meetings include two or three practitioners, family and friends of the client, and anyone else they want to invite.

Also involved in these network meetings are peer support workers who have lived with the experience of mental distress.

It's important to reiterate that it's the client who defines who will be included in the network meetings. My colleague described that underpinning Open Dialogue is that "mental illness is social and it's not prescriptive."

The network meetings help to support the client and their network to reach their own understanding of what they want. It provides a safe place without stress or anxiety, but participants have to be willing to engage. Mental health workers also reflect within the meetings. Everyone's views are respected.

This approach is very transparent and works with family, friends, and social networks in the client's home. Nothing takes place behind the client's back and any discussions about support and treatment options take place in front of them.

I feel that Christopher had treatment imposed on him and he didn't have any control. As a result he refused to engage with the mental health services. He had no safe place to express how he was feeling or what he wanted. Discussions about his treatment often took place in his absence. At times I think he was just resigned to the fact that he didn't have any control over his life anymore.

Whether Christopher would have been willing to engage in new therapeutic inventions I will never know. If you are a parent reading this who has a child with mental health issues, I would certainly encourage you to look at other interventions and not just medication. Most importantly, empower your child to have more control over their life and treatment options.

A few years ago I discovered mindfulness. It has been well researched over the last 30 years and has shown benefits in a wide variety of physical and psychological illnesses. It is used in the treatment of generalised anxiety disorder (GAD). It helps people to overcome anxiety and reduce tension in their body. They begin to understand their thinking patterns and learn how to deal with difficult emotions.

Mindfulness has its roots in Buddhist meditation and is a method of mental training. Instead of being on autopilot and rushing our way through life, it is about being fully aware in the present moment. We often spend our time either ruminating on the past or worrying about the future. Being mindful means we become very aware of and pay attention to our surrounding environment, what we are doing, and what is happening right now. We focus on the emotions, thoughts, and sensations we are experiencing. These include sights, sounds, smells, and tastes – moment by moment. Indeed by naming our thoughts it gives them less power and we learn to be in control of them instead of them being in control of us. We learn to catch our negative thinking patterns before they have time to take hold. The idea is that this results in us becoming less reactive and more calm. By practising mindfulness, you can improve your mental wellbeing.

When we pay attention to our thoughts and feelings, we learn not to judge them and become more compassionate towards ourselves. My grief of losing Chris comes in peaks and troughs, some days it hurts like hell and other days everything feels pretty much fine. My grief is ever changing.

Mindfulness is not all about clearing your mind and emptying it of all those thoughts that are constantly flooding in. It's about having an awareness of your thoughts, noticing them, and letting them go. While grieving, I have slowly incorporated mindfulness into my daily life. After a lot of practice, I am now able to become aware of the thoughts that often flood my mind. After noticing them, I accept and acknowledge them, let them go, and remain focused on the present moment and whatever task I am currently doing. Mindfulness is not a religion; it is a practice and it has now become part of my spiritual journey.

I am currently pursuing a diploma in mindfulness based stress reduction (MBSR), which I am thoroughly enjoying.

Chapter 11

~

What I Have Gained From Writing This Book

One question I'm often asked is what I have gained from writing this book. In some ways it has given me back my son. After he died, I spent so long ruminating about his illness and his death and trying to make sense of my loss, that I suppressed all the good memories about Christopher. They were just too painful to think about. Now I'm able to remember Christopher as a happy little boy and a quirky teenager. I truly believe that he walks beside me every day of my life.

I have moved forward since losing Christopher but life will never be the same. I want to remember the world he lived in and I want people to talk to me about him. I don't bottle up my emotions anymore and I've learnt not to apologise for my tears. I believe it is important as a bereaved mother to be kind to myself.

Losing a child is a very solitary journey and I have now joined some online bereavement groups which have been a great source of comfort. I've found it has decreased that sense of isolation bereaved parents often feel.

I set out to write this book to honour Christopher's memory and that's what I've done. People who have long-term mental health conditions can learn to effectively manage their symptoms and lead meaningful lives. Mental health services now employ peer support workers who have live experience of mental health issues and are a great support to service users. I have now become more focused on my work as a mental health nurse and life coach. It's so rewarding when my clients begin to take control of their lives and make positive changes. I try to create an openness about mental health and help people recognise their problems early. Taking care of your mental health is just as important as taking care of your physical health.

The two are often connected
Unfortunately, some well-meaning people will encourage you to stop grieving and get on with your life. This may happen because they can't cope with the pain of your grief. Everyone reading this who has lost a child will be at different stages in their own grief. Unless you have lost a child, it's difficult to understand how it really feels. Don't let people tell you how to grieve, but learn to embrace your feelings and emotions. Please do it in your own time and in your own way. Every bereaved parent's journey will be different. No matter what the cause of your beloved child's death, it's important to remember that you are never alone. There are organisations and other bereaved parents out there who can support you for as long as you need them. There are groups on Facebook for bereaved mothers and parents where you can talk freely and openly where only members can see who's in the group and their posts.

A personal note
Surviving the death of my son has been an arduous journey. In the early days I hid away and only did what I needed to get by. I was consumed with guilt and believed it must have been something I had done or failed to do that had robbed my son of the chance of a good life. Could I have somehow foreseen and prevented his death? I was very angry towards myself and felt a

failure as a parent. At times I was also angry towards my family and friends. But mostly I was angry with Christopher for dying and leaving me in so much pain.

Apart from my dad and Con, I felt there was no one around me who understood what it was like to lose a child. Mitch had simply walked away and I couldn't understand how he could be so cold and heartless. Just as my dad had supported me during Christopher's illness, he was also there for me after Chris died. He became my lifeblood and I clung to him for strength. I was constantly on edge and lived in fear that something terrible was going to happen to Elizabeth. I would panic if she was late getting home from work or I couldn't reach her.

As time went on I started to feel I owed it to Christopher to move on with my life, otherwise his would have been pointless. Meeting Steve reinforced that to me. He wanted to know all about Christopher and got to know him through me.

I know my journey is ongoing and sometimes something will trigger a memory and it will suddenly make me feel overwhelmed. It can be as simple as seeing daffodils on the side of the road. My best recommendation is to simply embrace those feelings, and trust that they will pass.

The pain of losing Christopher has lessened, but it will never completely go away. To be honest, I don't want it to. If you belong to a faith, I understand that losing a child can be a big test, but my spiritual beliefs have been very important to me. I know that he will always be in my heart and with me in spirit. Knowing that has helped me to find the strength to honour Christopher's memory. Many of the bereaved parents I talk to find it important to celebrate their child's life. It's part of the healing process.

I miss Chris dreadfully. The pain never goes away but I cope with it better now. Simple things, like a certain song on the radio, can trigger really painful emotions. Sometimes it can feel like a tidal wave coming from behind and it just lifts me off my feet. I've learnt to recognise that this is going to happen sometimes and there is nothing I can do to stop it. And I remember the feeling will pass, eventually.

It's important not to forget the grief of your child's surviving siblings. They have lost a brother or a sister and are hurting too. Although some children want to talk about the loss of their sibling and how they are feeling, my daughter didn't want to talk about it. I learnt to not force her to talk about it if she didn't want to. I was worried about how Elizabeth would take it when I told her about this book, but she has been very supportive.

Compassionate Friends holds annual worldwide candle lighting celebrations. I light candles at home to celebrate Chris's life and so does Elizabeth. I also contact other bereaved mothers who live locally. We take photographs and share them amongst ourselves. It feels so spiritual and uplifting, and shows me I am not alone.

It's important to remember that it's ok to move on with your life and it doesn't mean that you are leaving your child behind or forgetting them. They will always be an important part of you. Just learn to be gentle with yourself.

I do not belong to any organised religion but do have very strong spiritual beliefs, which have sustained me during the really difficult times. I do believe in a creative force some know as God and I know Christopher's spirit lives on. I was christened in the Anglican Church, but have no experience of this. In the 1980s I was drawn towards Catholicism, but after studying it for almost a year I found I could not commit fully to its doctrine. However, I did assimilate some of its teachings into my own philosophy of spiritual life and whenever I need to find some comfort, I always go into a Catholic Church.

As I continue my journey, I talk about Christopher all the time and don't want people to feel sorry for me or find it uncomfortable when I do. I will celebrate his birthday and remember him on Mother's Day. I will relive happy memories and laugh about the good times we had.

Chapter 12
~
Managing My Grief
The Bereaved Parent

The night Chris passed away I was surrounded by an invisible cloak that protected me from the trauma of loss. I felt a strange numbness that some people may see as denial. At the hospital I found myself trying to comfort everyone else and make sure they all had a lift home. The worst part was leaving the hospital. Despite the numbness, I couldn't bear the thought of him lying in the morgue all alone and his beautiful body being cut open during the autopsy that was to follow. I tried very hard to put that picture out of my mind and centre my thoughts on believing that he was now in spirit and at peace.

Later, after Mitch had gone to bed, I sat in silence, alone with my thoughts. Trying to make sense of what had happened. Unbelievably I still hadn't been able to cry. Perhaps that was because it would have made his death real. It must have been about 3 AM when something amazing happened. I felt a sudden sense of stillness and calm which I can only describe as a spiritual experience. The room where I was sitting suddenly felt strangely warm and was filled with a glowing white light, as if I were surrounded by angels. This lasted for about an hour and I found it really comforting.

I knew that my beautiful boy was being escorted on his journey to heaven. He had come to tell me that he loved me and was at peace. I had always believed in an afterlife and that night definitely confirmed it.

The numbness only lasted a couple of days. The pain of losing Chris has been overwhelming at times. A few days after he passed away I was sitting in the doctor's waiting room in floods of tears. The reality of his passing had finally hit me. I was overcome with raw emotion. I wasn't even aware of anyone around me until a lovely lady sitting opposite handed me a tissue. She didn't ask me why I was upset but I really appreciated her kindness. A few minutes later, I sat with a lovely doctor sobbing hopelessly. I felt a physical pain that was eating away at the pit of my stomach. My emotions had completely overwhelmed me and the realisation that my son was "dead."

To be honest, coping with child bereavement has been hard work. Elizabeth once said to me, "I know you wouldn't kill yourself, you wouldn't do it to me."

Her statement made me feel awful because I had thought about taking my own life several times during the first few months when the pain of being a bereaved mother felt too much. Black moods would descend over me and I just didn't want to live any more. How was I supposed to go on without my son? Life at times felt quite meaningless. However, she was right. I could never do that to her. She had already lost a brother, how could she cope with losing her mum as well? My beautiful daughter gave me a reason to go on. At times I would get very angry and question the fairness of it all. I would see parents whose children were the same age as Chris and I'd feel quite resentful. I would ask "Why me? Why my son?"... Which would inevitably end in my feeling awful about having such terrible thoughts about someone else's child.

For the first few months after he was gone my stomach was in knots. I felt sick and couldn't eat. Everything I tried to eat tasted like a brick. I lived on a sparse diet of mashed potato and tomato soup.

I felt so guilty after his death. I blamed myself for his mental health problems. If only things had been different when Chris was born and I had been able to bond with him sooner. I struggled to forgive myself. I would lay awake at night reliving the past. I truly believed in my heart that I had failed him, if things had been different he would have lived. Especially as the autopsy report revealed that his substance misuse and prescription drugs had contributed to his death. He died of liver and heart failure.

This would add to the intense pain that washed over me and sometimes I would hit the self-destruct button with a bottle of wine to help me sleep. I know it wasn't a good thing to do, but sometimes I just wanted to escape from reality. It was all too much to bear.

After meeting Steve I would often break down and tell him about the guilt I was feeling and that it was my fault that Chris had died. We would talk for hours about why I felt responsible for my son's death. He would tell me to stop blaming myself but I struggled to do that. Elizabeth would tell me that it was Chris's "time to go" and nothing I did contributed towards his death. I just had to find a way of letting go of the guilt that was continuously eating away at me.

When I had a breakdown in early 2012, I knew I needed some specialist help. I was having symptoms of PTSD. I couldn't sleep and when I did manage to drop off, I would have very distressing dreams. I was having continuous flash blacks of the night Chris died. So, I started seeing a lovely counsellor called Olwen from Cruse Bereavement Care. During one session she asked me if I would bring some photos of Chris to the next session as she would like to get to know him. When I took the photos in the following week it was like he was there with us. I took a great deal of comfort from being able to talk about Chris as a real person. I spoke a lot about my guilt and the reasons behind it. It was a safe space to talk about my son and really helped me to understand that there was nothing I could have done to prevent his death. Gradually the feelings of guilt began to lessen. I now realise that the guilt eating away at me was a normal part of the grieving process. Although over time this has diminished, people often say to me I don't know how it must feel to lose a child and, to be honest, until you do, you really don't know how it feels.

Throughout my life I have experienced the bereavement of other people close to me, but the pain of losing my child was by far the worst. It's unnatural to outlive a child. The mourning process was longer and totally different. I would and still do have times when the grief would hit me like a tidal wave and totally knock me off my feet. I would constantly think about what Chris's future would have looked like and the "what ifs." People avoided talking to me about it because they felt awkward and didn't know what to say. Some made me feel uncomfortable talking about my child who had passed away. I would find myself apologising for upsetting them. I'm not asking anyone to take my pain away; just allow me to talk about him. I'm entitled to talk about Chris as normally and naturally as anyone would a living child. Nowadays I talk more freely about Chris and I explain that he is now in spirit. I'm not going to stop talking about my son just because it makes people feel uncomfortable. I'm sure they would feel the same if it was the other way round.

The loneliness of being a bereaved mother is unbearable at times. The grief would leave my head reeling and I often felt like I was suffocating. I would withdraw into myself and do battle with the dark thoughts. During the first year I had just come out of a relationship and didn't have a partner to share the grief with. I hated Mitch for the appalling way he had treated me following our break up, especially the lies he told about me. I questioned how I could have been with a man for 13 years who was so callous knowing I had just lost my son.

I am so lucky to have met Steve. I'm sure a lesser man would have found my grief too much to cope with and wouldn't have stayed around. He has spent hours listening to me talk about Chris and mopping up my tears. Although he never knew him in life, he feels that he has gotten to know him through me. This is the kind of love a grieving parent needs and makes me love Steve all the more

For me the loneliness of being a bereaved parent has been one of the hardest things I've had to cope with. I experienced a massive range of mixed emotions and feelings, often living inside my head because it was easier than trying to apologise to others for how I really felt. I lost Chris back in 2006, but nowadays one of the benefits of social media is that there are many support groups that can support you on your journey of grief. Many of them are run by other bereaved parents. They offer you the space to talk freely about how you are really feeling without fearing that you will be judged. I remember some insensitive person saying to me once, "For goodness sake aren't you over that yet?" How on earth was I supposed to respond to that? I felt like someone had stuck a knife into me. I'm just glad that person has never had to go through the pain of losing a child!

It's good to be able to talk to people who have suffered a loss similar to mine. I find them really supportive, they help with the loneliness, and I'm also able to give back to other bereaved parents. Over the last few years, I'm so grateful to have made several friends who are bereaved parents themselves and have followed a similar path to me. We support each other, often meeting for coffee and a natter.

As I moved slowly forward through the grief, I made a conscious decision that I didn't want Chris's life to seem pointless. I often light a candle and sit with my memories of Chris. I remember how funny he was and his wonderful cheeky smile. I am very proud of my son and wanted to do something that would be a legacy to his memory. One of the things I decided to do was to channel my love for Chris into my life coaching. It was good to have a focus. I so desperately wanted to do something that Chris would be proud of.

I also thought back to my teenage years as a new mum and how bleak the future looked to me then. If only I had someone back then to help me to find a positive way forward. Everyone has life experiences that can have a negative impact on their mental health and prevent them from moving forward in a positive way. Although I've gained a qualification in life coaching, I also have the relevant life experience and empathy to help empower people to take more control of their lives. I hope Chris approves of what I'm doing.

Although the grief of losing Chris will last for the rest of my life, I am not lacking in happiness. I love and miss him every day. I have learnt to cherish the memories I have of him and will always be his Mum. I feel so lucky to have a wonderful husband, a beautiful daughter, and a lovely stepfamily. I have finally found a way of living with the loss, while honouring the memory of my child.

For Those Who Won't Ask

Don't get embarrassed when I speak of him.
Don't act like he never existed.
I do have another child – His name is Christopher.
Asking about him won't upset me.
Your silence is worse.

Don't be embarrassed when I cry for him,
Don't look down when I mention his name,
Or change the subject because you feel uncomfortable.
I love to hear about your children –
I want to talk about both of mine.
I can't make any new memories
But I cherish the ones I have.

Don't change the subject when I remember him,
Don't be afraid to say his name.
I want to share his memory with you.
I want to share my memories of him
I am a proud parent just like you.
I am a proud parent – of two.

~ Carol Macey

Resources

I would like to encourage parents to seek help sooner. Learn to read the signs that are right in front of you.

Bereaved Parents of the USA
Provides a safe space where grieving families can connect, share stories, and learn to rebuild your life.
https://www.bereavedparentsusa.org/

Compassionate Friends UK and USA
Provides friendship, understanding, and hope to parents and their families going through the natural grieving process.
https://www.tcf.org.uk/
www.compassionatefriends.org

Cope Foundation USA
Connects individuals who have experienced similar losses by offering ongoing emotional support, spiritual and therapeutic programs, as well as appropriate resources and referrals.
https://copefoundation.org/

Child Bereavement UK
Help children, young people, parents and their families to rebuild their lives when a child grieves or a child dies.
https://www.childbereavementuk.org/

Eluna USA
Supports children and families impacted by grief, addiction, or suicide.
https://elunanetwork.org/

Facebook Groups
There are many groups on Facebook for bereaved mothers and parents where you can talk freely and openly where only members can see who's in the groups and their posts.

Heads Together UK
A mental health initiative spearheaded by The Royal Foundation of The Duke and Duchess of Cambridge supporting young people, homeless charities, and war veterans.
https://www.headstogether.org.uk/

The Lullaby Trust UK
Raises awareness of sudden infant death syndrome (SIDS) and offers emotional support for bereaved families.
https://www.lullabytrust.org.uk/

Mental Health America USA
Promotes mental health as a critical part of overall wellness, including prevention services and early identification and intervention for those at risk.
https://mhanational.org/

Mental Health Foundation UK
Their mission is to help people understand, protect, and sustain their mental health.
https://www.mentalhealth.org.uk/

Mind UK
Mental health charity here to make sure nobody has to face mental health problems alone.
https://www.mind.org.uk/

National Alliance on Mental Illness USA
Provides advocacy, education, support and public awareness so that all individuals and families affected by mental illness can build better lives.
https://www.nami.org/

National Suicide Prevention Lifeline USA
The Lifeline is a free, confidential crisis service that is available to everyone 24 hours a day, seven days a week; provides crisis counseling and mental health referrals.
Call 1-800-273-TALK (8255)

Rethink Mental Illness UK
Helping to improve the lives of people severely affected by mental illness
https://www.rethink.org/

Samaritans UK
If you need someone to talk to, they listen, don't judge or tell you what to do, volunteers respond to 100,000 calls per day
https://www.samaritans.org/

Sane UK
Provides emotional support by phone, mail, and text
Offers online peer led forum to share your experiences with others
https://www.sane.org.uk/

Substance Abuse and Mental Health Services Admin USA
SAMHSA's National Helpline is a free, confidential, 24/7, 365-day-a-year treatment referral and information service for individuals and families facing mental and/or substance use disorders. 1-800-662-4357
https://www.samhsa.gov/

The Good Grief Trust UK
Provides useful information, helplines, advice, and encouraging stories from others to help you in this most difficult of times and to find a way forward with your life.
https://www.thegoodgrieftrust.org/

Young Minds UK
Fighting for young people's mental health
Great resources for young people, especially children
https://www.youngminds.org.uk/

About the Author

Carol Macey works as a mental health nurse and Life Coach. A decade and a half after the death of her adult son, Christoher, she mustered the courage to share how and what she has processed to cope with her significant loss. Christopher experienced his first psychotic episode aged 19, when Carol was a mature student studying for a degree in nursing. In spite of the best efforts of his friends, family, and a supportive mental health team, Christopher continued to deteriorate over the next ten years until his unfortunate death from liver failure at age 29. *The Spirit of Christopher* details how Carol and her family coped with the aftermath of his passing, how her training in mental health has helped her cope with her tragic loss, and how the very personal experience influenced Carol to become a better health care provider.

In writing *The Spirit of Christopher*, Carol wanted to commemorate a beautiful life and leave a legacy to friends and family, yet also impart wisdom of a bereaved parent that might shine out to other bereaved parents or those whose loved ones are dealing with severe mental illness. Through her deepest sadness, Carol was able to transfigure her experience into something positive and perhaps give hope to other bereaved parents in an otherwise miserable time. In the very least Carol aims to raise awareness of and reduce the current stigma surrounding mental health issues.

Carol shares her personal life experience to provide a mechanism for others to better understand a child or family member who is dealing with an ongoing and/or serious mental health problem. Her personal story plays an impactful role in her life coaching, as she supports her clients through her very personal healing journeys.

To get in touch with Carol ~
rainbowcarolring@googlemail.com
https://thespiritofchristopher.com/

www.ingramcontent.com/pod-product-compliance
Lightning Source LLC
Chambersburg PA
CBHW061208070526
44583CB00025B/3167